Joy On the Same Page

The Art of Building Relational Intimacy

Joy On
the Same Page

The Art of Building Relational Intimacy

Dr. Al Sarno

QUANTUM SHIFT
PUBLISHING

For information about special discounts for bulk purchases, please contact Support@QuantumShiftMedia.com

Editing, cover, and interior design by Quantum Shift Media

978-1-955533-18-8 Paperback
978-1-955533-19-5 eBook
Library of Congress Control Number: 2023931997

QUANTUM SHIFT
PUBLISHING

Denver, Colorado

Dedication

I dedicate this book to the Lord Jesus Christ
and to the friends and family
who helped me find the way of relational intimacy
so that I might be more like Christ.

Endorsements

Relationships demand time and energy, whether that relationship is between a husband and wife, parents, siblings, or co-workers. While relationships are meant to be enjoyed, at certain times weariness ensues. There are many underlying reasons for weariness in relationships; miscommunication, ego, anger, and hurt, are just a few.

However, there is good news! In order to better understand each other and combat the fatigue within, this book comes to the rescue. Yes, it focuses on marital relationships, nonetheless, tactics learned from this book can certainly be used to bring healing to other relationships.

A true masterpiece, this book by Dr. Al Sarno reflects his many years of counseling experience and his heart for the hurting. The design of the book reveals how earnestly Dr. Sarno wants people to enjoy God and His gift of relationship. The ease of reading and implementing this book makes it a lucrative investment for now and future generations.

I pray that this book be a blessing in your life.

"The Lord bless you and keep you; the Lord make His face shine upon you, and be gracious to you; the Lord lift His countenance upon you, and give you peace" (Numbers 6:24-26). Amen.

—Dr. Benish Masih BSc, MDiv, Th.M, DMin.

Dr. Al Sarno has been my friend for almost 40 years. I have walked with him through many painful times. He speaks from his diligent study and out of his journey. He has been able to help countless numbers of people through both the written page and the spoken word. In *Joy on the Same Page,* Dr. Al communicates that joy is found in even the most difficult situations.

—Pastor Don Walker
Kansas City House Church Pastor and Prison Minister

Dr. Al has been part of my life for several years now. He is a testament to a life lived for Jesus. His studies, along with real-life challenges and experiences, have led him to a place to be able to teach and encourage others with the Holy Spirit's help. He works closely with many to bring them healing and hope through extensive counseling. I am thankful he serves our military families so faithfully. I am thankful to know him and get to do life with him. May his words in this book be a blessing to you!

— Pastor K'Lee Reynolds
Rock Hills Church Manhattan, KS

Dr. Al Sarno has been a part of educating biblical counselors at West Coast Bible College & Seminary for over a decade. He is academically qualified, highly gifted, and called by God to practically assist those walking through some of life's most difficult trials with the help of the Holy Spirit. He's been a blessing to our students and community, and I am confident that this book will be of great value to you in your journey!

—Dr. Kevin Harrison,
President, West Coast Bible College & Seminary

Dr. Al Sarno is authentic, gracious, wise, and joy-filled. He is a deep thinker, astute counselor, and knowledgeable professor. Dr. Al's greatest accomplishment is that he is a man after God's heart. His love for others to experience healing, refreshing, and joy is contagious. God is using his life to bring transformation to countless lives. Joy amid suffering is not just a pie-in-the-sky dream, but a lived reality, as seen through this book and especially in Dr. Al's life and work.

—Pastor Lacey Hartman
Rock Hills Church Manhattan, KS

Preface

Joy On the Same Page is written for those on a quest to have healthy, meaningful relationships. Every day, I counsel people in relational turmoil who have yet to learn how to meet their need for relational intimacy. Relational intimacy is a need. It involves engaging with God (Father, Son, and Holy Spirit), ourselves, and generally five to seven other people.

I call this the Relational Intimacy Process® because in counseling others, I have learned that most of us do not have our relational intimacy needs met, and the consequences are pretty negative. The toll of the need not being met is heartbreaking and painful. Working through the process of building relational intimacy, as you will accomplish in the book and this Workbook, will bring healing from the pains experienced in life. The Lord has shown us these precepts in Scripture, and His way of healing is the best.

We lead busy lives, and our culture demands responsibilities that can take us away from our relationships rather than enriching and building them. Relationships require constant care, and *Joy On the Same Page* gives you tools to help with that care in a fun and meaningful way.

The Workbook includes space to do the principles and activities that are discussed in the book. The principles, based on biblical Scripture, and the activities, based on my counseling experience, will help you practice those principles so that they become part of you.

xii | Joy On the Same Page

Here are some suggestions to get the most out of this book.

- Download and print out the *Joy On the Same Page* Workbook for you and what I call your Same Page Partner from dralsarno.com/book/workbook. You and your Same Page Partner are encouraged to have your own copies so that you can read the principles and do the activities on your own, then talk about them together. The principles and activities will teach you how to grow together. It is a learn-and-grow book for adults.

- It's best to practice no more than one principle and activity each day.

- This book is both reflective and active. It is structured to help you build principle upon principle to establish a firm relational foundation to do the work and fully enjoy your relationship.

- It is both a primer and a refresher book. If the activities in the Workbook sometimes aggravates you, pay attention because something in you is being triggered and needs a little extra attention. Self-reflection and growth require some grit.

- This book is designed to assist you in building a joyful and meaningful relationship with God, yourself, and your partner. Its intention is to help you learn so you can avoid mistakes, build a better future, and help others do the same.

Whether this book found its way to you through a seminar, a counseling session, a video, a friend, or the media, I welcome you to a new beginning.

Acknowledgments

I am grateful to our Lord and Savior, Jesus Christ, who created, saved, and kept me. I was like a sheep that kept wandering away. Many times He picked me up when I stumbled and held me close to Him so that I didn't lose my way.

I thank Don Walker, Bob Mumford, Derek Prince, Charles Simpson, Charles Stanley, Hans Seyle, Doyle Montgomery, Don LeMaster, Charles Spurgeon, J.I. Packer, and many others for teaching me what I share in the book.

I thank the thousands of clients I've worked with over the years for giving me feedback on what works and what doesn't.

Thank you to those who helped me in recovery to keep me clean and sober since October 1, 1985. They saved me from my lower self.

I thank Keren Kilgore, my editor and publisher, and the staff at Quantum Shift Media for making this dream a reality! I have been working on the concept of this book since 2000. Because of you, I can leave a lasting legacy that will bring healing, hope, and life to people who are hurting.

I am grateful to my grandparents, who came over from Sarno, Italy, in the late 1800s and settled our family in America, where we are free to worship the God of our choice.

I am grateful to those who founded this country for the pursuit of life, liberty, and happiness. I am grateful to those who wrote the Constitution and those like my dad who defended it over the years—our brave servicemen and women.

I am grateful to my parents, who taught me the principles of the Christian walk and taught me a solid work ethic.

Thank you to all the principals and teachers who spent time with me to teach me how to listen and pay attention actively and to love school and learning. I especially thank my favorite preschool teacher Mrs. Hudlett, my second-grade teacher Mrs. Sweet, and my high school teacher, Mr. Riggs, for igniting my love of learning and for your patience with me when I was a rascal!

Thank you to my undergraduate, graduate, and doctoral professors for teaching me how to be thorough and detailed in helping others.

Contents

Introduction

My desire is for you to be on the same page enjoying your relationships and spreading that joy with others. Applying these principles within your intimate relationships will help you learn about and live in relational intimacy. Work on these concepts either individually or with your Same Page Partner daily.

This book is not finished or complete until you finish writing it. Your contribution to the work will transform this book into a guide for you. Think of it as a collaboration. I wrote the principles and provided the activities, but your interaction with both will provide the experience that makes the book a living thing. The activities in this book are a guide to help you in your quest.

I have developed a specific approach to relationships called the Relational Intimacy Process®. This process involves relational intimacy with God, self, and others. After our physical survival of needing air, food, and sleep, our first need is relational intimacy.

In Genesis 1:16-17 the Lord warned Adam and Eve that if they ate from the tree of the knowledge of good and evil, they would die. They did not heed God's warning and ate a piece of fruit hanging from that tree. This tree represented intimacy with God, self, and others, and the consequence was a slow death of the physical (soma) body while the soul remained eternal. The shame they experienced and the self-inflicted pain of prickly fig leaves for coverings indicated relational intimacy was broken and unmet.

God, in His grace and love, supplied animal skins for coverings from the lamb's sacrifice for the remission of sins. In this way, God initiated a repair of the relational intimacy if they and the offspring following would agree and respond. The choice is ours.

A *need* is something we cannot live without. We cannot survive without air, water, food, and sleep. Relational intimacy is also a basic survival need. We were not created to be alone. Relational intimacy can only occur with understanding and practice. That's what makes this book a quest. It will help you learn the principles and practice them through the activities.

Just like the people of Israel, we live in passive intimidation due to not being relationally intimate with God, self, and others. The Bible referred to hard-heartedness or a heart of stone. Jesus gave us a heart of flesh to respond to Him in relational intimacy.

The way out, written by the author of Deuteronomy, tells us that if we seek the Lord our God, we will find Him (4:29). The same is true with intimate relationships, actively seeking relationship and meaning with God, self, and others. If you search for relational intimacy earnestly with your heart and mind, you will find them. The danger is that we live in a culture where our relational intimacy needs go unmet. Our desires like humor, sex, power, and communication get distorted and amplified, for example, the consumption of goods, food, pleasure, and even ideology. This distortion can lead to contempt and cause self-destruction. Learning how to fill that relational need much earlier in life would be best. According to research, most of our core beliefs and practices get embedded within us by the time we reach the age of 14.

Finding or creating relational intimacy isn't an easy endeavor. Our finest example of relational intimacy was the treasure buried with the ancients long ago–Jesus, who was resurrected from the dead and brought to life the precious gift of intimate relationships. His relationship with God served as an example of the ultimate intimate relationship. He didn't model a religion but rather a way to connect to others and God in a meaningful way. John wrote, "No one has ever seen God by the one and only Son, who is Himself God and is in closest relationship with the Father who has made him known" (1:18).

I invite you to seek the treasure of meaningful, intimate relationships with me. I will share stories from my own life to help you understand that even through trauma and abuse, we can all learn to experience profound, intimate relationships.

If you learn the principles and practice the activities, this book can also be your story of hope and healing. Relational intimacy can grow in any type of relationship. Apply these principles to friends, those who live nearby, or across cyberspace. You can create healthy relational foundations in a premarital, engaged or married relationship. Both happy couples and those struggling can use these strategies to help deepen or heal their relationship. The book guides your quest to the treasure of a strong, intimate relationship.

In many of our relationships, we are not experiencing joy by being on the same page. Most of the time, we are not even in the same book with those we want to connect intimately with. The term *on the same page* is often used in the technical and engineering industry and refers to making repairs or fixing a glitch from a schematic or plans. Coaches and players also use the terms for a team concept of winning. When people attempt to fix the problem, they may be in different locations, but all have the same technical manual. Then, in troubleshooting the problem, we can experience joy by being on the same page with one another to connect and correct the problem.

Joy On the Same Page principles is for families and stepfamilies. The activities are used as course development in homeschool programs, Christian schools, and independent learning systems. University students can learn from the principles and practice the lessons from social work to psychology in academic programs.

Allow this book to become your friend. You can repeat the activities as many times as needed. I recommend you go in the order presented in this book. Later, you can choose principles or activities that suit your particular need at a specific time.

You will find different applications for each lesson through the daily principles and activities. Stay open and remain fluid when practicing the activities or applying the principles. I cover the following general topics in this book.

- Understanding relational intimacy
- Building individual, relational intimacy with God
- Compliments to affirm yourself and your Same Page Partner
- Adding humor activities and hugs to daily habits
- Managing anger through draining its reserves
- Learning to compliment your partner in front of others
- Money and all its goodness and complications
- The role of timeliness
- A look at the four faces of Jesus
- The importance of healing
- The importance of celebration

Knowing that God created the heavens and the earth for us to enjoy promotes relational intimacy with God (Father, Son, and

Holy Spirit). When I behold the beauty and majesty of creation, I think, *Wow, I know the One who created it all!*

Being grateful for creating us and this cosmos needs to be a daily intentional time of relational intimacy with God (Father, Son, and Holy Spirit). I am grateful to the Lord for giving me life and creating my family and friends to enjoy life together in year-round thankfulness. Please read Romans Chapter 1, Genesis Chapter 1, and II Corinthians Chapter 1 with this in mind. You will learn how relational intimacy causes the believer to thrive. We see this in the fact that most catechisms refer to the creation mandate of fellowship with God. I refer to fellowship as relational intimacy, as exemplified in the life of Christ. Gain a perspective in life that is a gift from Him in our daily journey. Relational intimacy is indeed our daily bread. Jesus said that man cannot live on bread alone. Relational intimacy is essential for our survival.

You and your Same Page Partner can both experience the joy of growing together in a healthy, balanced relationship. Everybody wants to increase the joy and decrease the tension within meaningful relationships. *Joy on the Same Page* offers you just that. It's possible to start this book alone to begin the journey to learn how to create and navigate intimate relationships on a personal level. If you have a partner, your personal growth will affect your relationship even if your partner is not engaged in the activities. *Joy on the Same Page* is a tool that can be used in many different relational settings and circumstances.

My hope is that this book becomes a relational cookbook with the principles working as an ingredient list and the activities serving as the step-by-step process of creating the dish. Now let's get started by learning how to enjoy relationships by being on the same page.

Chapter One

Getting Back
To the Garden of Eden

Understanding Relational Intimacy

John tells us that Jesus prayed, "that they may be one, even as you, Father, are in me and I in you that they may also be in us, so that the world may believe that you sent me" (17:21). This is a fundamental principle in life. If Jesus desired that we all become one with him and the Father, then we would be wise to make every effort to learn how to do so. God created us in His image; therefore, we are relational creatures; He placed that desire inherently within us.

Relational intimacy is the one need we must meet as we meet the other survival needs of air, water, food, and sleep. Meeting our basic survival needs of air, water, food, and sleep keeps us alive as survivors. But to advance to thrivers in our lives and deepen our lives meaning and purpose, we must learn how to chase relational intimacy despite the fear or boundaries we place around ourselves as protection. Jesus is our protector. The Old Testament tells us to "be strong and courageous. Do not be afraid or in dread of them for the Lord your God is the One who is going with you. He will never fail or forsake you" (Deuteronomy

31:6). This means that God has got your back. He will supply the courage you need to pursue relational intimacy. And when it gets difficult? He has promised not to fail or forsake you. Adam and Eve enjoyed perfect relational intimacy in the Garden.

There are over 52 activities and desires that sociologists have found that human cultures universally express, things like play, money, sex, culture, music, language, speech, competition, and humor that we enjoy throughout each day. The 52 universals fall into the *desire* category. We have 52 universal desires as humans. We are individuals in varying orders, preferences, and strengths, and it is helpful to convey these individual differences to each other in relationships.

There are 52 sociological, universal desires in every culture:

Adventure	Holding/Caressing	Reading
Appreciation	Honor	Relating
Beauty	Humor	Reproduction
Building	Improving	Risk-taking
Communication	Inventing	Serving
Competition	Joy	Sex
Connecting	Language	Significance
Creativity	Legacy	Skin Hunger/
Curiosity	Love	Touch
Dance	Loyalty	Speech
Daring	Meaning/Purpose	Speed
Debate	Money	Storytelling
Drawing	Music	Strengthening
Essence	Novelty	Structure
Exploration	Order	Taste
Fashion	Peace	Work
Forming Groups	Play	Worship
Happiness	Power	

What makes us unique can also pull us apart. If one likes listening to music and you do not, that is a potential disconnect. Or, if the type of music differs too much and we have a hard time with a compromise, we fail.

Some time ago, a study was done on couples happily married for more than 15 years, and they reported that the most attractive link that held them together was sharing outside interests and hobbies.

Each of us has a different order of preference for the 52 desires and different strengths of each on a scale of 1 to 10, which means the odds of two people having the same order and strength of preference are astronomical! So we need to be flexible and give people their *me time* to express themselves in their way, preferences, and talents.

Notice sex and physical intimacy are desires, not needs. We can live without them. True needs are limited to five and directly related to life sustainability.

Only one of those five is God's heart for us and is the purpose of this book: relational intimacy.

The opposite of intimacy is intimidation, as I will show later. We have four old core beliefs that develop in childhood and bring about intimidation of God, self, and others. The opposing true beliefs bring about relational intimacy.

Age	False Belief	True Belief
5	I'm no good	I like me
8	I can't trust anyone, not even God, myself, or my parents, or others	I can trust myself, God and some people

10	I get what I deserve	Begin to notice all the good things
12	Anger is bad	Anger is good; it shows I care
14	Addictions, self-destructive behaviors, self-harm I am my enemy	Self-care, self-nurturing, self-awareness I am my friend

If someone is raised in an intimate environment, or goes for counseling to change the old beliefs into new ones, the beliefs will become quite different. And the outcome at age 14, or from counseling, is quite different as well. By age five, we learn the concept of "I like me." By age 8, we advance to, "I can trust God, myself, and some others." By age 10, we are able to recognize a larger world outside of ourselves and feel optimism, "Good things happen for me." But sometimes, along the way, we pick up beliefs that are not healthy or based on truth. The anger belief, for example, becomes *anger is good; it shows I care,* and we pick this up by age 12. And then, when we turn 14, the relational intimacy need is met, and we must spend the rest of our lives maintaining it with joy. Rites of passage in many cultures, usually at age 13, are intended for the young adult to receive and practice relational intimacy.

Removing Resentments that Destroy Relationships

However, many of us have resentments that build up in a relationship, the relationship can be destroyed, even in childhood. The physics law of entropy applies to relationships and resentments, just like rust, destroys. So much so that what

I call entropic re-enactments work on annual cycles just like clockwork. If an Adverse Childhood Experience (ACE) occurs first at age 7 and it goes untreated, resentment of the event will self-sabotage you at 7 years of marriage, 7 years on the job, when your kids turn 7, and so forth.

The mid-brain memory banks start negative forecasting in high gear for survival and protection from the event it thinks will happen again, then self-fulfilling prophecies start to come true and foolish decisions follow, which wreak havoc on our lives.

In 2019, after 25 years of research on ACEs, the CDC defined ACEs as "Adverse Childhood Experiences (ACEs) are potentially traumatic events that occur in childhood. ACEs can include violence, abuse, and growing up in a family with mental health or substance use problems. Toxic stress from ACEs can change brain development and affect how the body responds to stress[1]."

We all need to be on guard of this, but especially people in recovery, as they might relapse in the 7th year of sobriety, for the example above, due to entropic re-enactment. Other folks may start getting panic attacks or depression. Some may start a new addiction. Some will be unfaithful in their marriage.

As an adult, preventative care is to deal with the ACE event(s) and remove the resentments with forgiveness so that the cycle can be resolved. Processing the anger and built up resentments is most critical so that in time healing can begin. Some people experience healing without full recall of the ACEs. Others who have obsessed about the ACEs stop having intense recall as the process of forgiveness unfolds.

---

[1] https://www.cdc.gov/violenceprevention/aces/index.html

Here I might emphasize the saying "forgive and forget" is an unreal expectation and is the shortened version of the original saying, which is accurate. "Forgive and forget to bring it up again." As Hans Syle, the originator of applying the engineering term stress to humans, wrote in *Stress without Distress*, of the various brains in our head, part of our brains will remember, but the higher thinking brains can apply forgiveness as a salve for healing.

The maxim I give my clients is: Know your ACEs! Forgive your ACEs!

Two Belief Windows: Intimidating and Intimate

When we are deprived of relational intimacy because we lack the experience or knowledge to give or receive it, we become both an intimidator and intimidated. We see that in story after story in the Bible, like David after the sin with Bathsheba or Moses when he struck the rock in rage. Some of us have lived it as well in our stories. When we live under this type of pressure of being intimidated, our lives and relationships sour. The literal meaning of intimacy is *to relate closely.* The root word is *tim* from which we get the word *time* that means *to relate.*

For a literal example, consider the earth in relationship with the sun. The prefix *in* means closely. The word *intimidate* has the same root and prefix with the additional syllable *da ro* remove. So intimidate means to remove close relating and is seen in many of the stories in Scripture. We intimidate with money, sex, porn, cigarettes, alcohol, drugs, anger, and so forth to deal with the pain we are in due to the panic of the relational intimacy need going unmet. we panic when our needs go unmet. That panic ruins the previously mentioned 52 activities we like to express in life.

There are two windows we can look out of as we experience life. The intimidating beliefs or the intimate beliefs. I counsel people to learn to look out the intimate window. It is hard to make the change as whatever we learn in the first 12 years will require *unlearning*, and humans tend to resist change. We can change, but it is most difficult.

The Intimidation Window

The opposite of intimate is intimidate. The Italian-American household I grew up in was chaotic and loud. Everybody debated everything. That may be why I am a debative learner. I must debate to learn, which can be exasperating for other people. And I like talking a lot, and unless I'm in session or teaching, it's not always in a soothing, comforting way. I like to be loud and contrary by nature. I like to stir things up. It drives people away and is by no means Christlike. People wanted to be around Jesus. While that is past tense as to when He walked the earth, it is still true today. As we are Christlike, people like to be around us, so they still want to be around Him!

However, I was blessed enough to have two loving teachers in my youth. Mrs. Sweet was my second-grade elementary teacher, and Miss Moppin taught my Child Evangelism Fellowship. As a child, I was a Tigger. I was highly energetic and talked all the time. In school, I was sent to the principal's office so many times I thought I was the principal. It's possible that many people in my adult life would still consider me to be a Tigger.

We are to intimate, and that is difficult for Tiggers to do. Intimacy is of God; intimidation is not of God. We are not to use intimidation in our relationships, ever. "Do unto others as you would have them do unto you," is the rule of intimacy. You can only fulfill that rule if you are intimate with others and yourself.

"Love your neighbor as yourself." The rule of intimacy means I never dominate, intimidate, or manipulate. Those are actions of intimidation. The thief, our enemy, and everything of his rebellion who comes to steal, kill, and destroy is the one who dominates, intimidates, and manipulates. That has been his tactic since the Garden of Eden.

Remember that spiritual warfare is fighting off the urges of envy, revenge, greed, and many others to not intimidate but rather to be relationally intimate instead. Taking every thought captive means refraining from domination, intimidation, and manipulation in a relationship and instead being loving, complimentary, and complementary.

Yielding to the Holy Spirit instead of to our flesh is doing spiritual warfare. The Joy of the Lord is our strength, and joy will fill us as we are intimate. Righteousness, peace, and joy flee when we intimidate. However, righteousness, peace, and joy fill us when we are intimate. We advance the Kingdom of God when we are intimate. We grieve the Holy Spirit when we intimidate.

So to respond in a relationship to bring about intimacy, we have to look out the new window. We pray, "Thy will be done on earth as it is in Heaven." We pray for relational intimacy to abound! May we walk in the Spirit and show forth the fruits and gifts of the Spirit! Consider the following verses as interpreted through The Message.

1. "But what happens when we live God's way? He brings gifts into our lives, much the same way that fruit appears in an orchard—things like affection for others, exuberance about life, and serenity. We develop a willingness to stick with things, a sense of compassion in the heart, and a conviction that a basic holiness permeates things and people. We find ourselves involved in loyal commitments, not needing to force our way in life, able to marshal and direct our energies wisely" (Galatians 5:22-24).

2. "God's various gifts are handed out everywhere, but they all originate in God's Spirit. God's various ministries are carried out everywhere, but they all originate in God's Spirit. God's various expressions of power are in action everywhere, but God Himself is behind it all. Each person is given something to do that shows who God is: Everyone gets in on it, and everyone benefits. All kinds of things are handed out by the Spirit and to all kinds of people! The variety is wonderful: wise counsel, clear understanding, simple trust, healing the sick, miraculous acts, proclamation, distinguishing between spirits, tongues, and interpretation of tongues. All these gifts have a common origin but are handed out one by one by the Spirit of God. He decides who gets what, and when (I Corinthians 12:4-11).

The Intimacy Window

It was a common pedagogy at that time to use physical force against students to punish negative behavior. Many of my teachers smacked rulers on my hands held on the desk. Some teachers hit my knuckles with the flat part of the rulers; others hit my knuckles with the ruler's edge. Some had me stand in the corner alone. It didn't matter if it was public school or private school; it seemed that my boisterous behavior irritated those around me, which usually ended in my humiliation or pain. These experiences were so profound that I did not own a ruler until I was in my thirties.

But Mrs. Sweet and Miss Moppin taught me a different way to alter disruptive behavior. They would simply put a hand on my shoulder and bend close and whisper, "Now, Jimmy, you can listen to what I am saying." Or "You can do better than that."

Sometimes they even praised me with, "You are such a good boy; let me see you listen." They both chose to speak into my life with intimacy no matter how much my behavior affected the classroom and their lessons. I know I was not an easy student. I was misbehaving and always moving. I spoke fairly constantly and could be a mischievous rascal. I had ADHD, no doubt, but back then, they called it PIA Pain in the A**. The doctors told my parents to give me rum to calm me down and help me sleep, especially after all the surgeries I had at two years old. I liked rum - a whole lot!

But not so with Mrs. Sweet and Miss Moppin. I knew they loved me, and they smiled each time when they saw me. Their hugs were like being touched by an angel. I thank the Lord for them. I got lucky again in high school with another favorite teacher, Mr. Riggs. Like Mrs. Sweet and Miss Moppin, Mr. Riggs used a gentle, intimate approach to teach and guide me. Their kind and personal approach worked for me. And the way they treated me was so powerful that I have modeled over 30 years of my educational pedagogy from preschool and early childhood education to university teaching after the three of them. Their approach to guiding and teaching even influenced me as a counselor. After decades in this field, my style is thanks to three teachers who chose to teach and mentor me with love and intimacy. But, in my relationships, I didn't do as well.

As a husband, I would fall short. I was a better version of myself inside my career than I was inside my home. It was this lack at home that caused me to begin the quest to find intimacy. I needed to live fully in both realms of my life. This book, in part, is drawn from all my personal and professional failures, including marriages.

With effort and discipline, I have learned to experience the Lord within an intimate relationship because He has taught me as the intimate One that He is. Think of this book as a treasure map to find intimacy. It can teach you how to fulfill the universal need for intimacy. Like you, I have looked for meaningful relationships in all the wrong places, in all the wrong ways, so use my experience as your guide.

We are designed to be relationally intimate with God (Father, Son, and Holy Spirit) and self. It is within these relationships that our intimacy needs can be met. In addition to God and ourselves, we need a circle of friends with whom we can intimately share.

Research by John and Julie Gottman shows that a healthy number of friends to relate with falls between 5 and 7 intimately. This range allows us to closely relate and share anything and everything about ourselves without fear of reprisal. And research isn't the only source for choosing these numbers. When Jesus walked the earth, He chose six people to relate to him in his inner circle. Peter, James, John, Martha, and Mary Magdalene and Mary were the six relationally intimate others and the closest of all the disciples.

By Jesus' example, our relational intimacy needs can be met. We can be back in the Garden of relational intimacy through Jesus Christ. It's important to note the distinction between relational intimacy and sexual desire. Relational intimacy is a need, while sex is a desire. It's easy to conflate the two because sexual relationships can feel very intimate. But intimacy and sex are not synonymous. Let's look at an example of relational intimacy. When Jesus lived on earth in human flesh 2,000 years ago, He chose to relate intimately with God (Father and Holy Spirit), Himself, and his inner circle of six others. Yes, He managed a larger circle of twelve male disciples and eight female disciples (perhaps fewer were needed since women generally talk more than men). He equally distributed his relational intimacy inside His inner circle between males and females. He associated closely with Peter, James, and John, as well as Mary, Martha, and Mary Magdalene. These three women were close enough to him to stand guard at his tomb, which made them the first to witness that it was empty. They were the ones who ran to the twelve disciples proclaiming that Jesus was no longer in the tomb but had risen according to His prophecy.

It is important to remember the cultural time and climate in 33 AD. Women did not hold positions of authority, so it is significant that three women bore witness and then served as heralds of this astonishing news. In that day and time, had the disciples made up the story about the resurrection, as they were falsely accused, they would not have had women be the principal players; the men would have been.

Further, the Lord's will is for all of us, male and female, to have access to God (Father, Son, and Holy Spirit) in intimate and meaningful ways. One way to think of being intimate with each the Father, the Son, and the Holy Spirit is to consider Paul's letter to the Romans. "For the kingdom of God is not eating and drinking, but righteousness and peace and joy in the Holy Spirit" (14:17). Some biblical scholars have delineated righteousness as from the Father, peace from Jesus who was prophesied by both Isaiah and Ezekiel as being Prince of Peace, and the Holy and Joy Spirit bringing joy are relationally intimate with the three in One.

Paul's words have a long reach as he implores us to be relationally intimate with God (Father, Son - Jesus Christ, and the Holy Spirit) and ourselves. And, like Jesus, we too can choose 5 to 7 others to enjoy life on an intimate plane. In my life and work, I have realized that most of us were not taught any of this, nor do we have contemporaries or those before us who modeled it. For me, my first taste of relational intimacy was found inside three of my school classrooms. But beyond that, I had no clear path toward imitating the principles my teachers taught me through love and acceptance. Consider I Corinthians 8:6 and II Corinthians 3:17, which discuss the role of each of the Trinity. I Corinthians 8:6, "yet for us, there is only one God, the Father, from whom are all things, and we exist for Him; and one Lord, Jesus Christ, by whom are all things, and we exist through Him" and II Corinthians 3:17, "Now the Lord is the Spirit, and where the Spirit of the Lord is, *there* is freedom."

PTSD Kills Relational Intimacy

Relational Intimacy heals PTSD! In all my years practicing counseling, I have come to find these two contradictory truths to be true. But it also describes the struggles of the recovery process. PTSD destroys the very thing we need to heal from PTSD!

Once we accept this truth, true healing can begin, and the healing process is enabled. PTSD is triggered by relational intimacy as the fear of intimacy, even though that same relational intimacy would heal the symptoms of PTSD. So how to resolve this paradox of healing?

Embrace the pain! We are already in pain with PTSD. Embrace the additional pain of seeking to fill relational intimacy to remove the pain and the symptoms of PTSD. We do not want to get close to anyone as we have PTSD. We practice avoidance. We are in that pain. So, embrace the additional pain of getting close to someone, and the pain of PTSD will dissipate. Then as we continue, the pain of getting close to someone will dissipate, and now, we are not living in pain any longer as long as we do not lash out at that person!

See, fear of intimacy is pushing people away. People who can help us heal. Pushing people away does not keep us from pain; it intensifies the pain. Embrace people and embrace the pain for the pain to go away. This is far less pain and costs than the pain of pushing people away. Besides, pushing people away makes them think they have done something wrong when they have not! Someone I pushed away ended up killing herself, and I still live in that pain. Pushing people away is the most common symptom of PTSD and is the most devastating to the person with it and to those around them. We were made to relate to people, not push them away. Our biology, physiology, and anatomy are made by God to embrace people and to enjoy life with people!

Embrace people to embrace joy.

As human beings, we need to be relationally intimate, which means we need to experience joy on the same page. Once we learn how to live with joy, we recognize the need and learn how to meet the needs of others. When we choose to look out the window of intimacy rather than intimidation, we practice living with joy on the same page.

Intimidation

There are four components of relational intimacy

1. To spend time
2. To self-disclose
3. To compliment (great job) and complement (differences in style are good)
4. To enjoy the mystery of relating. Why do we love those whom we love?

Yet, often we miss the mark, and intimidation sets in like entropy, as decaying matter. When the synergy and creativity from our relationships is depleted, we falter.

There are four components of living under intimidation

1. Avoid, hide, con
2. Denial, deception
3. Criticize
4. Become rigid or chaotic

Further, intimidation styles come in four packages; indirect as in social aggression, bullying, and cyberbullying; active, which manifests as abuse; passive also known as the silent treatment or stonewalling; passive-aggressive, which involves tone, subtextual communication default, meaning we have not learned another way to relate so we imitate what we have observed or experienced. What a dilemma we are in! We resort to behaviors that further thwart us from meeting our number one need. We sometimes even try to intimidate God. We push Him away or say He does not exist. Pretending He does not exist is intimidation, like telling someone they are worthless and do not matter. We intimidate ourselves with self-destructive behaviors and relationships. We sometimes intimidate others in any of the four ways mentioned. Our panic heightens as our need for intimacy is not met, and we self-destruct. We misuse our other four needs: we overeat or undereat, we oversleep or undersleep, we add harmful chemicals to our body, and then we misuse our 52+ desires to self-destruct somehow. We turn that which is good into bad upon ourselves.

Intimidation causes us to be alone, just ask Adam and Eve. Imagine their pain of going from intimacy with God, self, and others to intimidation and being alone. It was quite a fall.

The same is true for the couples I counsel who are married and alone. Being married and alone is worse than being single and alone. But the Lord does not want us to be alone in life. Suppose we are taught how to be relationally intimate by age 14 as God intended. In that case, our life would have a much different trajectory than if we had not been taught how to be relationally intimate. Look out the new window to meet the need. II Corinthians 5:17, "Therefore if anyone is in Christ, *this person is* a new creation; the old things passed away; behold, new things have come."

Only relational intimacy can help us live full lives of meaning and connection, and we must be taught how to meet this need. It cannot be automatically learned or acquired. It has to be modeled for us. Only then can we practice it and eventually learn it. Because of Jesus Christ, the desire we have is to teach what we have learned. In my self-disclosure of intimacy, I want others to learn from the errors of our ways, Yet I want to do so in such a way as to not self-criticize nor shame or condemnation since that would be intimidating. Because of Jesus,we want you to learn and practice the art of relational intimacy with your Same Page Partner in the same manner. Romans 8:1, "Therefore there is now no condemnation at all for those who are in Christ Jesus."

Relational Intimacy in Marriage

I confess that I have not attained all the hopes, goals, and desires of marriage. I have enjoyed moments of relational intimacy though I have not sustained these moments with another. I have had several attempts at marriage. While I had wedding ceremonies, I did not have a clue about marriage or relational intimacy.

To wed means to come together in an attempt to be one. Marriage literally means to be merry as I age = merry-I-age = marriage as then two become one.

I have enjoyed attending many Renewal of Vows ceremonies and have cried at them all. I feel such a reward after months of counseling a couple and guiding their healing from the trauma of intimidation to intimacy. To watch them express their love in a Renewal of Vows fills me with wonder and joy. It is a privilege to see intimacy heal broken lives. So, I cried at the ceremony. What can I say? In fairness, I cry at Hallmark movies as well. For some of us, our lives are like Hallmark movies, and for others, we are like Lifetime movies. No matter what, I firmly know that the Lord works all things together for good.

But, before being at that step of merry-I-age and joy, one needs to see and be taught what a good marriage is. Parents are to teach us how to be good spouses and good parents with relational intimacy. Thus, one might be a good parent or have had a good parent, but was that good parent first a good spouse to their spouse? Some of us who have experienced marital failure had parents who didn't divorce yet did not exemplify a good spouse to each other. They simply tolerated each other, or worse, hated to be together and weren't even close to living with joy on the same page. They were not even in the same manual. They were together but functionally divorced. Remember, we are still responsible for the now, though we still cannot do what we have not been taught.

Yet, despite what has been modeled for us, we are each individually responsible for what we do in the now to change the future. Hence, you have these teachings inside this book. We must learn to identify what was not taught to sustain and enjoy our relationships. We must learn to understand what went wrong in order to stop the cycle. What could we have done differently?

Identifying What Went Wrong

In November of 1985, Pastor Don Walker and his family took me into their home to bless and minister to me. I was at one of the lowest points in my life after getting clean and sober following the suicide of my second wife. I met my second wife in Fort Lauderdale, Florida, on holiday. I was there to erase the images of my first wife, who I found in bed with my best friend. I was taken by the woman at the bar and, in the throes of rejection and confusion, I married her a short time later. So, it was a rebound marriage. In May of 1985, following her suicide, I went on a self-destructive binge for months. I spent a disproportionate amount of time in a particular bar in Overland Park, Kansas. It became a habit to go in after work. I became friendly with the DJ, Doug Dimmel. He was the worship leader at Full Faith Church of Love in Kansas City, Missouri, where Don Walker was the Pastor. Doug and I would talk about the Bible and Jesus while I would get drunk or sit there high on drugs. He knew I was a believer who had lost my way and could see I was in tremendous pain. DJ modeled love and acceptance and helped to show me the way back to Jesus.

I was such a mess. I was only 29 years old, married twice, divorced once, and widowed by a suicide that I blamed myself for. Yet, Doug invited me to church, and finally, after I had overdosed and been in rehab, I accepted his invitation. I sensed the Lord near me while in rehab, and October 1, 1985, was my first day clean and sober since my first drunk when I was three. Remember the rum and how I like it in my childhood? Because Doug, and then later, Don chose to pursue me with intimate love, I could get up off the floor of my life and begin to walk again.

Living with each other with joy on the same page is crucial. It is not in a rigid, controlling way but in a loving, caring way. There are many names and labels for what I hope you accomplish in this book. I avoid those names and relations since adult learners often tend to project the past onto the current, and misperceptions occur. We even do it in annual cycles that are marked by childhood trauma ages.

Please note that I could not write this book had it not been for the many people who taught me these principles. You see, I have been on both sides of the couch and on a lifelong quest with many others who have shared with me the truth and life of Jesus in relational intimacy. Though a counselor, I have been in rehab three times and been in counseling off and on for periods of my adult life. I have been an active member of many churches and heard many wonderful, inspiring sermons. As a student, I attended many colleges, seminaries, and universities. Later, I even taught some hoping to apply these principles and tasks and to pass them on before I go home to be with the Lord at the Marriage feast of the Lamb. I look forward to seeing you there, too. But while we share this earth, let us commit ourselves to the pursuit of relational intimacy in joy.

I have learned there is a big problem, and it is one we hope to avoid in our relationships as well. Humans are slow to change our perceptions and preferences. Unfortunately, relationships are all about learning and change, so we must overcome this problem. I know that some people avoid counseling because of misperceptions of what it is all about. Some think it is going over the past and trying to change things that cannot be changed. Some think it is a waste of time. Going to therapy is scary until we learn that it is simply about learning to change and heal. Counselors teach us to adapt and cope. With guidance, we can learn to enjoy life. We must make an effort to sort out all the junk we have been through and not project that junk into the future. We can learn to project the precious things forward while we cast the junk aside. It has not all been junk; there are precious things to pass on.

Chapter Two

Relational Intimacy with God

Becoming a friend of God is what the love letter, the Bible, is all about. The Bible is a rulebook as we start to get to know God, and then as the years go on, we see it as a love letter from God. The world's longest love letter is the Bible, and as we read it, we start becoming a friend of God.

God is love, and love is an action, creating and being love. Love grows as time goes on as we learn from God to become loving and a friend of God. He is to be our best friend as we grow in relational intimacy with God (Father, Son, and Holy Spirit), ourselves, and others. The key people in the love letter, the Bible, were said to be friends of God.

Jesus the Son was such a friend to God that He said, "If you have seen me, you have seen the Father." The Godhead is a friendly, functional, healthy, fun family of love! God lets us decide how close we want to be, though He draws us closer in love. If being a friend of God is something that interests you, then spend time with Him, compliment Him (praise and worship), and read about Him in the love letter, the Bible, which He wrote for us and gave to us.

Oh, and in the making and writing of that love letter, there are stories of people who sacrificed their lives, were abused and persecuted and hated and mocked so that we could get that love letter from God. Not to mention the shining pinnacle of that love letter is that the Son died a horrific death as an expression of the ultimate love for us that God so loved the world that He gave. He became broken so we could become whole. By His stripes, we are healed. We have forgiveness, and eternal life offered to us because of His death, burial, and resurrection! The laws of the universe were altered, and a new covenant was ushered in!

He changed the laws of the universe in those events. The old covenant became the new covenant. He made a way for us to become His friends in greater numbers. Only three or four had been His friends in the old covenant. When He started the new covenant two thousand years ago, He started with 12 to 20 to a hundred, then thousands, and now thousands. I'm talking about being friends. Many more are saved and could be friends with God if they want to be. The choice is ours to respond to His love.

The Bible is a beautiful book. It is a beautiful love story, full of love stories. In the beginning, the God of love, who is love, creates in love Adam and Eve to enjoy love with each other and with God in a Garden called Eden. This arrangement was meant to last for eternity. But Adam and Eve mess things up along with Satan, and God drives them out of Eden. God sets a course correction for humanity on Sinai mountain, in Gethsemane Garden, on Calvary, and finally in Heaven. Love prevails, and then the Bible ends with a Marriage Feast of the Lamb, our Groom, with us forever. We, as the bride of Christ, will enjoy eternity with God, the relationally intimate Three in One God of Love. Some folks have a hard time believing this story, and so did I before God touched us to become the bride of Christ, and we responded to His love. Yes, bad things happen to us, but love prevails. We can enjoy relational intimacy with God, ourselves, and each other, no matter what.

Generosity and Relational Intimacy

Some people were raised to be frugal, so it may be difficult for them to be generous. However, when you find people in recovery, you will find a generous person! Why is that?

Well, we have been given another chance in life and are enjoying life, so we want others to enjoy life, too! So, we are quite generous! Yet, at times, we find ourselves being resentful when others are not generous as well! Frugal or stingy people irritate us. I think it is quite evident in the creation of God around us that He is not frugal or stingy but rather a God of abundance and not of scarcity! One seed of any fruit, plant, or tree produces more seeds in the millions! One grape seed produces many vines with many grapes that contain many seeds!

There are areas in the universe that astronomers call star nurseries, as so many new stars are produced in that area. New stars. Think about how many stars there are! And yet more stars are being created! All to the glory of God and to encourage us to be generous like He is!

One way we can tell if we are relationally intimate with God (Father, Son, and Holy Spirit), ourselves, and 5 to 7 others, is by how generous we are. When we are generous, we are relationally intimate, yet when we are not generous, it might be because we are not relationally intimate.

To know someone is to be like them. Our God is quite awesome in every way and especially in generosity! To know Him is to be generous like Him! He is still creating stars for His and our pleasure! I like that about our God; He can never have enough stars! They are pretty cool, and so is He!

Enjoy!

Intimacy with the Trinity and Myself

"To this end we also pray for you always, that our God will consider you worthy of your calling and fulfill every desire for goodness and the work of faith with power, so that the name of our Lord Jesus will be glorified in you, and you in Him, in accordance with the grace of our God and the Lord Jesus Christ" (II Thessalonians 1:11-12).

When Paul wrote this letter to the Thessalonians, he was encouraging them to stand firm in their relationships with God and each other. He was responding to reports of false teachers who were tugging at the new church in ways contrary to God's plans. He wanted them to fully nestle into their own giftings to fully understand the goodness of God. Basically, he was instructing them on how to have an intimate relationship with God the Father and God the Son.

Intimacy with God is an awesome experience. Many people think of spiritual intimacy as experiences reserved for occasional spiritual highs. We know that relational intimacy with God is a daily, awesome experience. Further, we enjoy intimacy in a mysterious way with Father, Son, and Holy Spirit - each in a unique way, yet three in One. Hence, the first principle of intimacy is intimacy within the Trinity and within myself in His image. That is truly an awesome mystery of being. It is a mystery that is to be enjoyed though unsolved, simply enjoyed. Being able to embrace mystery is a sign of health and balance.

Finally, remember: He wants to be intimate with us, more than we want or even realize. Because He is Intimate, He will not intimidate, so He waits for us. In Paul's letter to the I Corinthians 8:3 he says, "But if anyone loves God, he is known by Him." In seeking God and listening for Him, we can be certain that He knows us. As we draw near to Him, He will draw near to us. Lord, help us to enjoy being on the same page with one another. The Lord lovingly created us to have a relationship with us and for us to relate to each other.

Practice - Intimacy with the Trinity and Myself

Pray this prayer with me:

> *Lord, I ask for a revelation of who you are and who I am. I pray for a revelation of intimacy with you, God, that is fresh and new. I ask to be drawn closer to you and not be scared away. God, reveal Yourself to me in this way and for my Same Page Partner. Amen.*

Then, Download and print out the *Joy On The Same Page* from dralsarno.com/book/workbook and answer these questions:

- List three ways your relationship with the Father is different from your relationship with the Son
- List three ways your relationship with Son is different and from your relationship with the Holy Spirit.
- List three ways your relationship with the Holy Spirit is different from your relationship with the Father.
- Pray for understanding, then read John 14. Write down what you notice about how Jesus spoke to His disciples about His purpose in this Chapter.
- Write down what Jesus says about the purpose of the Holy Spirit.

- Write down any misperceptions you may have about the distinctions between God, Jesus, and the Holy Spirit.

- Choose three times throughout the day to listen to God's voice and write down what you heard each time and try to distinguish which voice belongs to God the Father, Jesus the Son, and God the Holy Spirit. Job 33:14 says, "Indeed, God speaks once, or twice yet no one notices it." So be diligent and vigilant when listening for His voice.

Finally, remember: He wants to be intimate with us, more than we want or even realize. Because He is intimate, He will not intimidate, so He waits for us. In Paul's letter to the Corinthians he says, "But if anyone loves God, he is known by Him." In seeking God and listening for Him, we can be certain that He knows us. As we draw near to Him, He will draw near to us. The Lord will help us have joy with our Same Page Partner because He lovingly created us for relationships..

Six Types of Prayer

"If you ask Me anything in My name, I will do it" (John 14:12-14). Intimacy with God occurs as we spend time praying. I Thessalonians 5:17 tells us to "pray without ceasing." This is possible as we meditate upon Him and His Word and pray for others. There are six types of prayer. We remember these with the acronym A.C.T.S. M.E. We will discuss each type in detail.

A is for adoration of the Father, Son, and Holy Spirit. When approaching our God, our Father, in prayer, it is good to start with Adoration of Him and who He is! Adoration is a response of love in putting Him first.

C is for confession of truth as declaration and confession of sins as repentance. It is good to confess the truth and then to confess our sins. The word confess means out loud. No secrets, no shame, out in the open. Ready for forgiveness and healing.

T is for thanksgiving for all He has done and what we have. Be thankful for the forgiveness and healing and all the other joys and appreciation you have in your life.

S is for supplications or supply requisitions for what we need. Ask for what you need. Even though God already knows and has provided, He wants us to ask to deepen the relational intimacy with us and with Him.

M is for meditating upon His Word and waiting to hear His voice. Pause and quietly listen for His still small voice for Him to speak to you. I have found that the Father, Son, and Holy Spirit have different voices that I can discern as I listen and meditate upon Him and His Word.

E is for exaltation of our God. End the prayer time with exaltation of the Lord, let us exalt His name forever! Exaltation is acknowledging Him above all else. He is above all. And all things mean all things! Consider Psalm 70:4, "May all who seek You rejoice and be glad in You. And may those who love Your salvation say continually, 'May God be exalted.'"

A.C.T.S. M.E. prayers are throughout all the Scriptures and especially seen in the Psalms. The 23rd Psalm and The Lord's Prayer follow this pattern even in order of the acronym. God wants us to communicate with Him. He wants us to be intimate with Him. We compliment Him to be intimate with Him. That is what praise and worship genuinely do in our relationship with Him.

A is for Adoration

I Chronicles 16:29, "Ascribe to the Lord the glory due to His name." Revelation 19:7, "Let's rejoice and be glad and give the glory to Him, because the marriage of the Lamb has come, and His bride has prepared herself." As a bride adores herself for her husband-to-be, we are to adore the Lord in all His beauty and might.

Practice - A is for Adoration

Using your *Joy On The Same Page* Workbook that you downloaded from the website, do these exercises:

- Underline what stands out to you in these verses. I Chronicles 16:29, "Ascribe to the Lord the glory due to His name." Revelation 19:7, "Let's rejoice and be glad and give the glory to Him, because the marriage of the Lamb has come, and His bride has prepared herself."
- Write down two things you adore about God.
- What are three ways you can express your adoration to Father, Son, and Holy Spirit, and why they are meaningful to you?
- Share those ways and why they are meaningful to you with your Same Page Partner. Ask your partner to share theirs with you.
- What did you learn together?
- Together express adoration to Him.

C is for Confession

"Therefore, confess your sins to one another, and pray for one another so that you may be healed" (James 5:16).

C for confession of truth as declaration and confession of faults and wrongs as repentance. Confession is first described in the Bible as a declaration of truth. Eve was shamed by Satan and then sin, wrongdoing, and intimidation followed as seen in chapters Genesis 1 - 3. Satan shamed her and intimidated her into making a false confession. The poison of shame did its evil work and they sinned to try to cover up and change things with a false confession. If they had stuck to the truth and not believed a lie, things would be a whole lot different. Of course, we would have done the same thing. The things we try to do to change the lies are often harmful to us. And when we believe the lies we suffer and languish, Rather we flourish when refuting the lies with the truth in the Word of God as Jesus did in the desert temptation (see Matthew 4).

The antidote to the poison of our dilemma of shame is grace. The more we confess the truth and the more we believe the truth, the more abundant life we enjoy. Yes, suffering comes. Though if we declare the truth and we act in the truth, the suffering becomes our tutor, teaching us to be like Christ. If we believe a lie, for example, that we deserve the suffering or that God doesn't love us anymore, we can make a bad situation worse.

When faced with a bad situation, we can either make it better (intimate) or make it worse (intimidate). Confess the truth for healing and intimacy to come. The bad situation is due to our sin or someone else's but either way, if we allow God to become an intimate partner, He will be glorified through the healing of that sin. Remember Jesus speaking in Chapter 9 of John? He was healing a blind man and His disciples asked who was at fault for the blindness, the man himself or his parents. Jesus said, "It was neither that his man sinned, nor his parents, but it was so that the works of God might be displayed in him" (John 9:3). We need to respond in all situations with truth and grace. When we sin, we need to quickly run to God and not away from Him to find grace and help in times of trouble. If we confess the sin, He removes the sin and shame. When someone sins against us, we need to quickly forgive. Yes, we can remain angry, and forgive at the same time. Remember Paul's instructions, "Be angry and yet do not sin" (Ephesians 4:26). Someone's sin against us will make us angry. That is a natural reaction to betrayal against us. But if we seek to have an intimate relationship with God, then we must follow his requests. He has asked us to forgive those who trespass against us. If He has created hardship, like blindness in Ephesians, so that his work might be displayed in the healing, how much more will He display his work in our healing? Relational intimacy with God has to do with confession, which means to speak out loud, tell, or say.

Practice - *C is for Confession*

- Write down 5 truths you want to declare and confess each one out loud.
- List two sins that habitually trip you up.
- Share these two lists with your Same Page Partner.
- Write down anything that surprised you.

Enjoy the truth and learn to let go of the shame of the sins. While grace is not a license to sin, He (our Grace) died and rose again so we can be free from the full effects of sin. He died so we might live. We long to live in joy and be on the same page with Him and each other.

T is for Thanksgiving

Colossians 3:15, "Let the peace of Christ, to which you were indeed called in one body, rule in your hearts; and be thankful."

T is for thanksgiving. It amazes me that we can appreciate so little about ourselves. In my years of practice, I have seen so many people who don't know how to celebrate or love themselves. Even people who are wrongfully "in love with themselves" as opposed to healthy self-care or think that they "are all that" are insecure about who they are. They have formed an illicit bond with themselves because they didn't appreciate how God made them to begin with. For me, when I begin to bloat with self-importance, my unthankful attitude leads to me-worship. When we understand how obedience to the Lord leads to thankfulness, our self-appreciation becomes God-worship. We didn't create the birds that bless us at our bird feeder but rather we thank their Creator, the Lord for them. We didn't create ourselves, and so we must thank the Lord for creating us.

We leave messes in life, yet we are not a mess. Look out the new belief window of intimacy and see yourself as a saint who sins yet is no longer a sinner as we are saved by grace as a gift from God. We are God's creation - yet because of sin, we are messes and all - for whom Christ died that those who believe and obey Him, should have eternal life. How can we not be thankful?!

Practice - T is for Thanksgiving

Recall the two lists from the previous lesson. Great job for doing all that work. Now you're going to focus on yourself. How do I like me? Let me count the ways.

- Write down five things you appreciate about yourself. Write down the first five things that come to mind with no qualifiers or diminishers. What qualities do you possess for which you are thankful? Remember to include the little things because they are not so little.

- Share your self-appreciation list with your Same Page Partner
- Ask them to add three more items to your list.
- Notice the long list you have and take a moment to be thankful to the Lord for YOU.

Supplication or Supply Requisition

"I will even make a roadway in the wilderness, rivers in the desert. The animals of the field will glorify Me, the jackals and the ostriches, because I have given waters in the wilderness and rivers in the desert, to give drink to My chosen people" (Isaiah 43:18-23).

S for supplication or supply requisition. Those of you who work in a corporation, a school, or in the military know all too well what a supply requisition is. It is a form you fill out and turn in to the supply depot so you may get what you need. Sometimes you wonder if it is even read or answered. Praying to God and listing our needs is like turning in a supply requisition only, with God, we know it will be heard and answered. What do you need to be relationally intimate with God, self, and others? If you do not know what you need that is a need. Put in a supply requisition to God. Ask and we will have, and remember, at times, we have not because we ask not.

Practice - Supplication or Supply Requisition

- List five recently answered prayers.
- Share with your partner and merge the lists - you should now have 10.
- Write down five things you like about praying with each other.

M is for Meditating

The way the Bible teaches that we are to meditate upon the Lord and His Word. I would invite and encourage you to meditate upon a verse the Lord leads you to that resonates with your life purpose every day for a week. Hebrews 3:13, "But encourage one another every day, as long as it is *still* called today, so that none of you will be hardened by the deceitfulness of sin." One day that verse jumped off the page after I had prayed for the Lord to show me how to be a better counselor. Another of my life Scriptures that He showed me early in my calling was Isaiah 61:1-3 showing His heart for people and how Jesus read it early in His ministry as a type of ministry vision:

1
The Spirit of the Lord God is upon me,
Because the Lord anointed me
To bring good news to the humble;
He has sent me to bind up the brokenhearted,
To proclaim release to captives
And freedom to prisoners;

2
To proclaim the favorable year of the Lord
And the day of vengeance of our God;
To comfort all who mourn,

3
To grant those who mourn *in* Zion,
Giving them a garland instead of ashes,
The oil of gladness instead of mourning,

The cloak of praise instead of a disheartened spirit.
So they will be called oaks of righteousness,
The planting of the Lord, that He may be glorified.

Practice - M is for Meditating

- List five Scriptures you think may be about your life calling
- Share with your partner and merge the lists.

E is for Exaltation

"I will exalt you and praise your name" (Isaiah 25:1).

Exaltation is the sixth type of prayer to be relationally intimate with the Father, Son, and Holy Spirit. Exalt the Lord and lift His name on high for the wondrous things He has done for His people.

We are free from sin, exalt Him.

We are free from shame, exalt Him.

We are free from hell, exalt Him.

We are free from addictions, exalt Him.

We are free from captivity, exalt Him.

Rejoice and sing His praises. Compliment Him. "Hear, you kings, listen, you dignitaries, I myself will sing praise to the Lord the God of Israel" (Judges 5:3).

He wants us to compliment (praise) Him since that action will draw us closer to Him and He draws near to those who draw near to Him. We were made to praise Him.

Isaiah 55:6-7, "Seek the Lord while He may be found; call upon Him while He is near.

Let the wicked abandon his way, and the unrighteous person his thoughts; and let him return to the Lord, and He will have compassion on him, And to our God, For He will abundantly pardon."

And in Psalm 7:17 we read, "I will give thanks to the Lord according to His righteousness and will sing praise to the name of the Lord Most High."

That is what we all want, to enjoy being humans who are close to God. He created us for His good pleasure to give us the pleasures He has put in our hearts. Contemplate the beautiful imagery of relational imagery in the Lord's promise to old and new Israel, "The mountains and the hills will break into shouts of joy before you, and all the trees of the field will clap their hands" (Isaiah 55:12).

Practice - Exaltation

- Write down 10 reasons you have to exalt God.
- Share your list with your Same Page Partner.
- Discuss the reasons you have in common and those that are different than yours.

Now we all are moving toward having joy on the same page. We are fulfilling our destiny and finding joy in the Kingdom of God.

Chapter Three

Compliment and Affirm Yourself

Complimenting Yourself

"Delight yourself in the Lord, and He will give you the desires of your heart. Commit your way to the Lord, trust also in Him, and He will do it" (Psalm 47:4-5).

There are many examples of complimenting yourself in Scripture. Jesus, the Apostles, the Song of Solomon and the Psalmists, and many others complimented themselves. At the same time, we are cautioned not to brag or boast about ourselves. Complimenting yourself is telling the truth about how God has gifted you and how you have obeyed the duties of that gifting. It is about stating how your interdependence on God and others has made you who are in Christ. Trust in the Lord as you proceed in the process of complimenting yourself to your Same Page Partner.

The Gottmans, leading researchers in marriage and family, found that we compliment ourselves to each other a great deal in the dating process, and then as soon as we marry we stop doing so and this may cause the passion to wane. Keep complimenting yourself to each other even after you marry. In fact, the Gottmans describe healthy families who compliment in a ratio of 5:1, five compliments for every one criticism in general.

Further, we are His friends. We have much to compliment ourselves about. Yes, we fail, yet we are no longer sinners but saints who sin. The name we have been called after gives us the right to be joint heirs and as such we want to guard our inheritance, which is the Kingdom of God: righteousness, peace, and joy in the Holy Spirit.

Relaxation is the remedy for chronic stress and is the most effective way to deal with life. Chronic stress stops us from seeing the good in ourselves and others. So it is critical to hear the voice of the Lord so that we rest in Him. Read Hebrews chapter 4 about the rest of our Lord.

When you feel stressed, read the Self-Talk Relaxation exercise out loud so your brain hears you tell it what to do. Try to build this habit of relaxation for three weeks to assist you in being relationally intimate with yourself and to hear from Him. After three weeks you will have formed a habit.

Self-Talk Relaxation

Deep muscle progressive relaxation.

Sit in a comfortable chair with armrests and let your hands drape over the arms of the chair. Have both feet on the floor about hip-width apart as is comfortable for you. Say the following statements out loud.

1. I feel quite quiet.
2. I am beginning to feel quite relaxed.
3. My feet feel heavy and relaxed.
4. My ankles, my knees, and my hips feel heavy, relaxed, and comfortable.
5. My midsection and the whole central portion of my body feel relaxed and quiet.

6. My hands, arms, and shoulders feel heavy, relaxed, and comfortable.

7. My neck, my jaws, and my forehead feel relaxed. They feel comfortable and smooth.

8. My whole body feels quite heavy, comfortable, and relaxed.

9. I am quite relaxed.

10. My arms and hands are heavy and warm.

11. I feel quite quiet.

12. My whole body is relaxed, and my hands are warm, relaxed, and warm.

13. My hands are warm.

14. Warmth is flowing into my hands. They are warm, warm.

15. I can feel the warmth flowing down my arms into my hands.

16. My hands are warm, relaxed, and warm.

17. My whole body feels quiet, comfortable, and relaxed.

18. My mind is quiet.

19. I withdraw my thoughts from the surroundings, and I feel peaceful and still.

20. My thoughts are turned inward, and I am at ease.

21. Deep within my mind, I can see and experience myself as relaxed, comfortable, and still.

22. I am alert but in an easy, quiet, inward-turned way.

23. My mind is calm and quiet.

24. I feel an inward quietness.

The relaxation is now concluded and your whole body is reactivated.

Breathe deeply and write the following phrases:

1. I feel life and energy flowing through my legs, hips, midsection, chest, arms, hands, neck, and head.
2. The energy makes me feel light and alive.

Stretch your arms up in the air.

Do this complete exercise daily for three weeks. Then, when stressed simply say aloud, "I feel quite quiet" and your whole body and brain will respond as if you had done the entire exercise.

Practice - Self-Talk Relaxation

- Write down 10 sincere compliments about yourself without diminishment or sarcasm.
- Read them out loud to your Same Page Partner.
- Listen as your Same Page Partner reads their 10 compliments to you.

Affirmation is a God-given blessing for us to have joy being on the same page.

Relating to Myself

Proverbs 3:5-6, "Trust in the Lord with all your heart and do not lean on your own understanding. In all your ways acknowledge Him, and He will make your paths straight."

How do I relate to myself? That is not an easy question to answer. Who am I? How do I die to me and at the same time avoid esteeming myself higher than I ought? What is the balance?

One of Satan's deception tricks is to shift the emphasis off of God onto me. This makes me falsely believe that all outcomes rest on my actions. That is religion talking and it stinks. I can't go anywhere without me allowing God to take me there. So, it is an interdependent thing. It is not all up to God and it is not all up to me. It is up to us, together.

In essence, God says "you made the mess, I'll help you, and together, we'll clean it up." This is the design He has set into motion since the fall of man. The fall of Adam and Eve took us away from constant close relational intimacy with the One true God, ourselves, and each other, your Same Page Partner. Now we are at odds and experiencing intimidation, so our relational intimacy needs go unmet. In consequence, we hate ourselves and our Same Page Partners.

But wait. How can we say we love God but hate one another? John, when he was quite old and perhaps therefore quite wise, wrote, "If someone says, 'I love God,' and yet he hates his brother or sister, he is a liar" (I John 4:20).

Our love of God will draw us to be relationally intimate with Him. We will then enjoy relational intimacy with God, ourselves, our Same Page Partner, and others.

Practice - Relating to Myself

- Write down who you want to be.
- Write down three ways you want to behave in order to be that person.
- Write down the 10 compliments again about yourself from above. Can you add any others?
- Write a thank you note to yourself for going this far to change into the person God wants you to be. Give the glory to Him. The glory is His and the compliment is yours.

- Pray and seek the Scriptures to see the difference between glory and compliment (praise). Share what the Lord shows you.

Practice Good Event Log

For the next three days, write down one good event that occurs for you or for those whom you love each day.

Chapter Four

The Four Cycles of Relationships

There are four cycles we go through in any relationship, whether relating to God, others, or ourselves. Bruce Tuckman [2]and Irving Yalom in their work were the first to identify these cycles though I have modified the order for conflicting systems and couples. Tuckman and Yalom found the stages to be *forming*, *storming*, *norming*, and *performing*.

The stages or phases in the cycles of high conflict systems between couples emphasize who is right and force their own will/norms upon each other without yielding to one another. In conflict, the storming phase, some relationships break up and so do not make it to the performing phase. Storming is an expression of anger and conflict. We have to be taught how to successfully make it through the storming phase. How to turn me into we for a joyous marriage.

Let's look at each phase.

---

[2] Tuckman, B. W. (1965). Developmental sequence in small groups Psychological Bulletin, 63(6), 384–399 https://doi.org/10.1037/h0022100

Forming Phase

When a relationship forms, each part or person changes. Even a relationship with ourselves, our body, soul, and spirit changes from glory to glory once we receive Christ and make Him our Lord. For example, when we receive Christ and make Him our Lord, dying to self becomes the process of change so we can love ourselves and like ourselves as He loves us and likes us. II Corinthians 5:17 says, "Therefore if anyone is in Christ, this person is a new creation; the old things passed away; behold, new things have come."

Some people get nervous at the idea of loving and liking ourselves. The reason people struggle with learning to love themselves has to do, in part, with understanding the difference between selfish self-love and honoring-self-love. The Bible can help us out here. In biblical Greek, there are two words to help make the distinction. The Greek word *sarx* means the flesh habits of self that oppose God. The *soma* or body of self that for now contains our body, soul, and spirit is created in His image and for His glory and is good. That new nature within our *soma* is what to like and love. Even the external shell, body, *soma*, is called the temple of the Holy Spirit in Scripture. Loving ourselves through *sarx* may manifest as vanity or arrogance. If we learn to love ourselves through *soma*, we will direct our gratitude or our gifts and awesomeness to God.

The problem we have in forming relationships within ourselves is understanding the difference between *sarx* loving and *soma* loving. And this takes discernment in the Spirit. Knowing when not to like and love takes discernment as well. Thus, there is a fluid both/and process, not a static either/or. It just isn't that easy.

In the Forming Phase, we overlook the love/hate aspect of all relationships. In early relationship forming, we tend to airbrush the other. Our brains want to minimize the defects or peccadillos and amplify the good stuff. We are polite and careful.

Practice - Forming Phase

This task will help you to explore the Forming Phase. It will challenge you to use some of that creative genius God gave you.

Choose one or more of the following to describe how a relationship is formed.

- Draw a picture with any choice of materials, sculpt some clay or Play-Doh™.
- Write a story or descibe a story, book or movie, Bible or otherwise that fits you.
- Sing a song that is your favorite.
- Show it or tell about it to as many people as you are comfortable, and tell the meaning behind your creative masterpiece/expression.

Norming Phase

Norming is where relationships progress in a dynamic way. We all follow norms or unwritten expectations that have been modeled for us by parents, peers, or God. Norms are like established and acceptable codes of behavior. I grew up having to say ma'am and sir as a norm. Some consider them rules.

I strongly recommend people abandon rules that are quite chaotic or against the flow of life God has for us, like doing your own thing. He is a God of grace and mercy who teaches us through order and boundaries. Thus, we need to find His balance in the truth, which rests between the extremes of the rule of no rules, which is chaos, permissiveness, or biblically called *antinomianism*. The word *antinomianism* means against the law, against knowledge, or against common sense. we can find the balance of being who we are in Christ as individuals in service to Him as He helps us find that balance.

In the Norming Phase, we establish codes of behavior or rules of conduct. These are necessary to build relational intimacy. However, there is a danger of creating relationships that are strangled by norms we set in place. We can have too many rules or become rigid without grace. The Bible discusses this phenomenon in Matthew. "Woe to you, scribes and Pharisees, hypocrites. For you tithe mint and dill and cumin, and have neglected the weightier provisions of the Law: justice and mercy and faithfulness" (23:23).

The church often refers to this type of behavior as legalism and can mean the worship of law, and not the giver. This extreme described in the Bible produces control freaks, which God is not. In the Norming Phase, we must find a balance between too few and too many norms. The Book of Galatians was written to those in the extreme of legalism to bring them into balance. The books of I & II Corinthians were written to those in the extreme of antinomianism to bring them into balance. The balance of norms to find intimacy is very difficult to achieve in our relationships. The importance of balanced Biblical living is also seen in the letters to the seven churches in Revelation 1 - 3. Notice how in the 60 or so years from the death, burial, and resurrection, to the letter being written, six of the seven churches had become off balance, three went legalistic and three went antinomian and needed to be corrected by Jesus. Only one church or perhaps two remained balanced in Jesus, the churches of Philadelphia and Smyrna. We need to live together with joy on the same page.

Practice - Norming Phase

Read Revelation 1 - 3. Then fill out the table in the Workbook to indicate how your relationships are norming. The reference to Described As (Name an animal) is a preview of the four faces of Jesus that we will discuss later.

Storming Phase

Meaningful relationships will experience storms, such as conflict and anger. It is how we behave within the storm phase that can determine whether we can grow together and rely on each other. For example, when a problem occurs, do you draw together and attack the problem, or do you attack each other and enlarge the problem? Most couples experience a good number of storms, the most common are concerning spirituality, sexuality, time, money, and raising children. Conflict is not a bad thing. When handled properly, it can produce character development, growth, and maturity in both people and the relationship. To do that, fair fighting is essential. There are four rules of fair fighting:

1. One person talking at a time. No interruptions or defensiveness.

2. Use positive I-statements, not accusatory you-statements.

3. No name-calling or voice-raising. Be polite, not criticizing.

4. Kind gestures, no harmful physical contact. The only physical contact is hugging not hitting.

I have two more suggestions that are more sound practices than rules.

- The bedroom is for courting so do not turn the bedroom into a courtroom. This means no fair fighting ever about anything in your bedroom.

- A moving vehicle is also off-limits for fair fighting, especially if one of you is the driver.

In general, it's best to stop all activities during an argument as they can distract, become dangerous, and often foster an environment for miscommunication. Heavy discussions while driving cause many miscues in nonverbal communication as we react to the responses that are more about what is going on the road around us than the content of the dialogue. So when we respond to a nonverbal expression, it may not be about what we are saying, but, rather about something occurring on the road. We mistake the nonverbals for what is being said, hence high miscommunication.

I used to get quite angry, even aggressive when I spilled something. Anger is good as it shows we care. However, displaying anger as aggression is not good. Negative displays of anger are quite a turn-off. There is nothing manly or macho about them

The word husband is synonymous with gardener. A gardener may get angry about weeds but will seldom uproot the weeds with such force that it uproots the vegetables or flowers as well. Care must be taken in pulling weeds. Anger must be contained.

There is no room for aggression by a gardener in a garden. A loving, healthy relationship is like a garden. There is no room for aggression in a loving relationship. Physical aggression (i.e. hitting, pushing, shoving) and social aggression (i.e. name-calling, passive-aggressive behaviors) are all off-limits in the garden of a healthy relationship. Anger can be expressed in a healthy way without aggression.

Aggression is a low-brain response to defend territory and life. Anger is an upper-brain response showing care for a loss or disappointment, expressed with careful words that do not inflict more harm. Husbands take care what you plant and uproot.

Anger expression without aggression is a procession of care and connection. Aggression, whether social or physical, severs the connection!

Practice - Storming Phase

- Write down five things that irritate you about how you handle and issue.
- Write down five things that irritate you about how your Same Page Partner handles an issue.
- Project five projects or events where you want to spend your money.
- Write down five lessons you learned about money as a child that cause you frustration.
- Compare lists with your Same Page Partner. Write down the differences.
- Consider four ways you can achieve harmony in your values concerning money.

Performing Phase

Performing is the glorious activity we anticipate in relationships. The relationship performs the calling and tasks called to do by the Lord! This is the phase we all want to get to. Think of any performance that brings joy. The church choir or a cantata, for example, performs and the sound is lovely. Maybe you like the symphony or theatre. Some people are musicians and can perform for themselves. When you enjoy a performance, you are blessed. So it is with relationships. When we perform well together, we are blessed. And what a glorious sound when we are in agreement, in the same key with joy on the same page.

The Bible tells us that it is glorious when we walk in unity. Paul tells the believers that people will know we are Christians by our love. A relationship that performs at its highest capacity is designed to bring joy to us and to our Creator. Paul tells us that this type of sacrificial love is like a sweet aroma. "Walk in love," he tells us, "just as Christ also loved you and gave Himself up for us, an offering and a sacrifice to God as a fragrant aroma" (5:2). The translation for "aroma" is "the odor of fragrance." A relationship that is built upon the principles of seeking relational intimacy is such a thing of glory that it produces its own fragrance.

Just for fun go to your search engine online, and search *gardens in the Bible.* See the significance of the garden and unity to our discussion here and throughout.

Psalm 133:1-3, "Behold, how good and how pleasant it is for brothers to live together in unity! It is like the precious oil on the head, running down upon the beard, as on Aaron's beard, the oil which ran down upon the edge of his robes. It is like the dew of Hermon coming down upon the mountains of Zion; for the Lord commanded the blessing there—life forever."

In my family therapy practice, I use AROMA as an acronym: Affection, Respect, Order, Merriment, and Affirmation. You have an AROMA exercise coming up! This AROMA concept provides the key ingredients to make a house a home and can transform co-inhabitants into a healthy, harmonious family.

Surviving, and then learning from the storms that inevitably come, requires a stable focus. James teaches that we must have faith and focus to overcome the storms. "For the one who doubts is like the surf of the sea, driven and tossed by the wind" (1:6-8).

Stability requires confidence and commitment to one course. A relationship riddled with fear or pettiness will not withstand the storms. We must learn to quash our own insecurities and our judgments against our partners' insecurities to resolve the wars within and without. Stability begins inwardly with reflection and self-love but it manifests outwardly.

Practice - Performing Phase

It's creative time again. Follow the checklist to make up and perform a scene with your Same Page Partner.

AROMA Exercise

- Write down one way your partner shows you affection.
- Write down one thing you respect about your partner.
- Write down one way you and your Same Page Partner organize and event (a date, a dinner party etc). For example, maybe you sit down over coffee and start a list. Perhaps you research restaurants or themed meals.
- Name one way you infuse merriment into your daily schedule.
- Offer a recent affirmation you gave your Same Page Partner.

Choose a setting for your scene

Choose from this list of prompts if you wish.
Your living room
A park

A haunted house
Your in-laws
A vehicle
A swimming pool
A bowling alley
If you are feeling risky, choose an abstract space.
Inside your refrigerator
Inside your brain

Choose a topic for the scene

Possible prompts
What would you like to be doing in ten years?
If you opened a restaurant, what kind would it be?
The best superpower
The best Christmas dinner
Favorite isle at the grocery store
What is your dream job?

Write the script

Use the AROMA worksheet to guide the play.
Example
Setting: A busy restaurant where you can't get service
Topic: What are the items in your handbag

You: You know, I really respect that you…..(from worksheet)

Partner: I respect prompt service but you can't always get what you want.

You: (sings) But you get what you need.

Partner: I'm bored, let's play a game.

You:	Okay, I have to guess three items in your handbag before the waitress brings us our menus.
Partner:	Deal.
You:	Lipstick?
Partner:	Too easy.
You:	Driver's license.
Partner:	Boring.
You:	Um…
Partner:	Uh, oh, here she comes with our water glasses and menus.
You:	I love the way you (fill in from Affirmation line on AROMA worksheet)
Partner:	She's here, dinner's on you Mister.

Accept Storms as a Normal Part of a Relationship

Storms exist in every healthy, dynamic system and relationship. Without presuming upon the mind of God, can we not reasonably say that a storm brewed between the Son and the Father in the last hours of Jesus' physical life here on earth? Starting at the Garden of Gethsemane until Jesus said, "It is finished," there was storming all around. One had to yield to your Same Page Partner and so Jesus the Messiah, the Christ yielded His will so we could have eternal life. And that we could enjoy life and life more abundantly starting now on earth. In other words, Jesus accepted His storms.

In 1981, I was in Fort Lauderdale, Florida for graduate school. I moved into an apartment on the second floor of a two-story building. One evening, several of us were in the living room playing board games. The winds picked and the skies turned gray, but, being Florida, we gave it no thought as that happened all the time. Suddenly with no warning, we heard a loud train sound and our ears popped. We looked around and immediately dropped to the floor. Then a roar became deafening and we heard loud crashing. As quick as it started, it stopped, filling our apartment with a calm and serenity all its own. I looked up and saw no ceiling or roof, only the sky. It was very dark. I got up to look around and saw all my stuff gone from every room and every closet. Shards of glass were driven in the drywall at about 6 feet and higher. Had we been standing, the shards might have found us.

We went outside and saw my neighbors, who told us that there had been a tornado flying through our neighborhood. The twister went down the whole length of the building and ripped off the roof and sucked up all our belongings. Indiscriminately, the tornado dumped some of them in the pool or into the Atlantic Ocean. No one died and for that we were grateful. But, all of our stuff was gone. It was fortuitous that I had renter's insurance to help recoup some of the losses.

But as with any household, the most precious items are the ones that hold little monetary value. We all treasure our sentimentals. For me, it was my tan linen disco shoes with orange translucent soles and heels that lit up when I danced. These were lost somewhere in the ocean and I would never be able to replace them. Gliding along the ocean floor with my disco shoes was my entire Grundig system with the professional turntable with the professional vertical tracking arm. And all my pictures were gone. Our apartment itself sustained major damage. The HVAC ductwork was flattened and exposed. It looked like the entire insides of the apartment had been ripped out and laid bare. Yet, even in all that loss, I remained thankful that no life was lost, not even anyone's pet.

I have counseled people who have lost a loved one in a storm and I understand their devastation. Relationships themselves, when they end poorly, feel much like the chaos and devastation of a physical storm. I would experience several relational devastating storms the next several years following 1981, including the ones I spoke of in Chapter One and a few others.

The presence of storms and devastations in relationships can anger us, frighten us, or discourage us. Often, they do all three. Yet, our perception of the storms is the key. God is perfect and yet we even storm with Him. When we learn to become thankful for the storms and the life they produce, as well as learn how to clear away the damage that occurs in the clean-up, then life abundant follows. Counseling will aid us in the process of healing after a devastating storm.

We all know the story Matthew told about the violent storm that sprang up while Jesus and the disciples were traveling by boat. The storm churned up waves strong enough to cover the entire boat. The men were terrified. Some of them were fishermen and held a healthy respect for the sea and even *they* thought they would die in the throes of the storm. Relational storms can feel that terrifying. They can become so emotionally violent we fear our relationship may not survive the damage. In Matthew, Jesus slept through the storm, He was never even bothered by it because He knew it would pass. When His disciples went below deck to shake him awake He was more annoyed than anything. "'Save us, Lord, we are perishing,' they cried out to Him. 'Why are you afraid?' He asked them" (Matthew 8:25-26). He reproached them for having so little faith. He wanted them to be assured that calm always follows the storm. Jesus chose to intervene in this particular storm and rebuked the wind and the sea which instantly calmed.

Jesus expected the storm, it was part of life, especially of life on the water. His sleeping didn't signify indifference but rather an acceptance. When we fight with those we love, underneath the anger, and possibly even stronger than the anger, is fear. We are afraid to be rejected, dismissed, or mocked. If we can learn to accept that storms will come, perhaps we can rebuke that fear and calm our own stormy seas.

Practice - Accept Storms as a Normal Part of a Relationship

- Write down the topic of your last argument.
- Write down the real reason you argued if separate from the topic. For example if you argued about leaving a cup in the sink instead of putting it in the dishwasher, perhaps the real argument was about you feeling taken advantage of or not feeling valued when it's your turn for dishes.
- List two things you learned from that argument.
- Name some fears you had during the argument.
- List two ways you expressed healthy anger.
- Write two things you wish to tell your partner about that argument.

Learning to Forgive as the Key to Performing

Battles or storms within a relationship often leave open wounds in the aftermath. We often say or do things we regret when tossed about in the chaos of the storm. In order to feel safe after the storm, we must be willing to evaluate our behavior. This often results in identifying behaviors or words that harmed the other person. Partners must acknowledge foul behavior and ask their person for forgiveness. In the froth of a storm, we very likely harmed the other and were harmed by the other. The only way to resolve and heal from these injuries is to ask for and receive forgiveness. We can once again turn to Paul's instructions to the Ephesians when he told them, "Be kind to one another, compassionate, forgiving each other, just as God in Christ also has forgiven you" (4:32).

Forgiveness is often misunderstood among Christians. It does not absolve the person who has inflicted the injury but rather frees the injured from carrying the weight of resentment and bitterness against them. In some ways, forgiveness has very little to do with the other person at all. It is an act of mercy that benefits the one offering the forgiveness.

Ok now for a paragraph of fun. I like me and we like us. Me like me. Me thinks me is great. Me am having fun telling me about how much me likes me. Hello me. What do you think, me? Do you need to forgive me At this time? Is me forgiving me as easily as me is forgiving everyone else? Why me? Why does me have such a hard time forgiving me? Who me? Yes, me. Forgive me since God Almighty has forgiven me, now so do I.

Practice - Learning to Forgive as the Key to Performing

Write a note to yourself forgiving yourself for any actions or thoughts that caused you or others injury. Use the following worksheet.

- Open the letter by saying a nice thing about yourself.
- State what you did wrong.
- Write why you are sorry. Be specific.
- End the letter with an affirmation for yourself.
- Share the note with your Same Page Partner.
- Tell each other what it feels like to forgive.

Guided Journaling to Genuine Relating

In 1985, after two suicides of people close to me and some other significant and traumatic events in my life, I re-evaluated the counseling I had both given and received. I noted that when I suggested a client journal their experience, they would stare at the blank page having no idea what to write. I found the same to be the case, as I was overwhelmed with grief.

This prompted me to develop the BEST IDEAS guided journaling format. I also wanted to integrate therapy with spirituality. In the early 1980s, this type of merging was unpopular. Some even considered it unethical. I chose to incorporate spirituality into my work anyway and am relieved to see that the social and clinical climates have become more amenable to this type of counseling. I want to share the BEST IDEAS journaling format here as it is a useful tool to learn to live together on the same page with joy.

The BEST IDEAS Format

1. **B**ehaviors. What observable behaviors do you want to change? (Limit to 5 total per day, increase humor as one of them. Humor helps us change.)

2. **E**motions. How do you want to feel about the new behaviors? (Write the obvious.)

3. **S**pirituality. What spiritual principle will help you? (Think ethics or morals, like, being kind to myself and others, if spirituality makes you nervous. Remember, spirituality is not religion.)

4. Thoughts. What new thoughts do you want to think? (Write the obvious. Include the new beliefs of the new belief window we discussed earlier.)

5. Interpersonal and Relations & Interdependency. Who can help you in this process? (The longer the list, the better.)

6. Drugs/Diet. What changes do you need to make in what you take in? (We have 52 diets in addition to food - think food and the others, like music, touch, play, work, money, sex, and humor.

7. Environment. What do you want from those around you to help you? (An example: Ever talk to someone and wanted them to listen and not talk, and as soon as they told you resented it? – Tell them before you talk, "I would appreciate it if I could just emotionally vomit while you listen until I get it all out and then we can talk to clean it up….")

8. Attitude. What will be your "attitude saying"? (Make up a creative personally motivational brief bumper sticker type positive attitude saying.)

9. Support. Will you stay positively and actively involved in your support systems? (Yes, or maybe equates success.)

Sometimes in life, I have been choking and drowning and the Lord has rescued me with a heavenly Heimlich or CPR to restore me to love and balance in Him. This work you are reading is a result of His life-saving revelations to me that He also wants to impart to you usually while journaling. Often revelation will come in the times of journaling and contemplation on Him and His glory and light. A truly wonderful sight that changes despair to beauty and depression to joy. He makes the crooked paths straight and the road less traveled more a highway.

Those of us with high ACE scores know the crooked paths and roads less traveled all too well. We have been left for dead as the life has been sucked out of us. It is why I believe there is such a fascination with vampires and zombies. They are a picture of how we feel and have been mistreated. Well, the Giver of Life comes along and with heavenly Heimlich or CPR to restore us, gives us new life and a new belief window to look out. Our relational intimacy needs are met, and we are filled with joy indescribable. People are no longer taking, but rather He is giving life.

In 1969 I was 14 years and received the Baptism of the Holy Spirit which I have come to understand as the beginning preparation of intimacy with the Holy Spirit, leading to greater intimacy with the Father and the Son, the three in one. I was just a kid, born and raised in Presbyterian churches, including Coral Ridge Presbyterian in Fort Lauderdale, Florida with a strong foundation in the Westminster Shorter Catechism Principles of Faith. I had to recite the Catechism at age 12 to be baptized and sprinkled. I loved biblically sound teaching even at a young age.

On one particular night, I was with the youth group from Calvary Presbyterian at a large inter-denominational service at a packed house, War Memorial Auditorium, at Holiday Park, in Fort Lauderdale, Florida listening to one of the speakers, Bob Mumford. The other speakers were Derek Prince, Charles Simpson, Ern Baxter, and Don Basham. We were listening to Bob preach the Word and at one point suddenly, the Holy Spirit fell, and we all began to speak in other tongues. It was phenomenal and beyond description. Looking back and comparing it to Acts 1-3, would be quite descriptive.

Performing in Joy as Praise and Worship

The praise and worship that went up that night was wondrous and the fragrance of the auditorium changed from a packed auditorium to a beautiful aroma of a garden of roses and gardenias. Believe me, as a 14-year-old kid I noticed all that, as it was so sweet. Following that time, we would pray for each other anywhere, even in the locker rooms at school, and the aroma in the locker room would go from, well, locker room, to sweet and beautiful. People were getting saved, and we had sunrise baptisms in the Atlantic Ocean. We needed it because as "Florida kids" our sins were so numerous, the whole ocean helped us picture God taking all our sins away as water baptism signifies obedience to the Lord.

Scripture plainly states in Psalm 27:6, "And now my head will be lifted up above my enemies around me, And I will offer sacrifices in His tent with shouts of joy; I will sing, yes, I will sing praises to the Lord." and in Hebrews 13:15, "God-pleasing sacrifices through Him then, let's continually offer up a sacrifice of praise to God, that is, the fruit of lips praising His name."

To understand it clearly and succinctly, in question and answer 1 of the Westminster shorter Catechism we read:

What is the chief purpose for which man is made?

The chief purpose for which man is made is to glorify God, and to enjoy Him forever.

Blessing to say out loud: May all we do be pleasing in the sight of God both now and forever! Amen

Chapter Five

Humor and Healing

Humor is Vital

Humor is vital to all relationships, not some, but all. We each have a sense of humor in varying styles and varying degrees. It is a muscle that needs to be exercised no matter what we are going through.

Like any other gift, humor when used properly can be a positive tool for coping with stress and dialing down stress levels. The amount of laughter you and your relationally intimate friends is a good indicator of how healthy the relationship is. Positive humor never puts anyone down and is never sarcastic or caustic. Joy fills the air when positive humor is used. The mood in the air is of gratitude for the joy experienced.

When one is anxious or depressed, the goal of seeking out positive humor is very important. Masking the anxiety or depression with negative humor is not the goal as it will only increase any undesired outcomes.

Take a moment to close your eyes. Take a few deep breaths. Picture a recent funny occasion or joyous event. Picture yourself laughing, and enjoy the sensations in your body. Open your eyes. Feel the joy wash in waves over you. Thank the Lord for giving you the gift of joy. Thank the Lord for providing you with those events of joy and laughter. Thank the Lord for creating play in our lives!

It is just as true that the family that prays together stays together and the family that plays together stays together. Pray, play, and enjoy!

Practice - Humor Is Vital

- Start a humor file.
- Read the newspaper's comic section online or print the funnies.
- Cut one out that relates to yourself and your Same Page Partner. Nurture the comic within.

Add comics to your file and encapsulate them over the next year, especially when stressed, fatigued, in conflict, or prior to a stressful event.

Humor Is Good Medicine

"A joyful heart is good medicine, But a broken spirit dries up the bones" (Proverbs 17:22).

Humor is good medicine. Learning to appreciate your sense of humor and your Same Page Partner's sense of humor takes practice. Humor comes in all shapes and sizes. Humor is good for the body, including for our six brains. Our brains like and need humor and need the neurotransmitters, endorphins, and dopamine, released during humor.

Try smiling really, really, really big, and at the same time, try to think a negative thought. Your brains fight off the negative thought to keep that smile going. Humor triumphs over negativity. Couples in conflict do not laugh together much and just reversing that trend could assist your marriage greatly! Merry-I-age!

Humor can include funny stories, quips, one-liners, comebacks, looks, motions, and more. Remember, we all have a sense of humor to be developed. Some of us have over-developed humor (hardly ever serious or always silly), and some have underdeveloped humor (always too serious or negative or critical or caustic). Humor in balance is a good thing. We need at least three good belly laughs a day, or ten hardy laughs a day.

Practice - Humor is Good Medicine

- Add five items to your humor file.
- Review the ones above and encapsulate their meaning here adding the date.

These can be funny mementos, jokes, stories, cartoons, or other items of humor. Work that humor muscle and watch it grow. You both want to experience joy on the same page even if your humor styles look different.

Remember to Have Fun

Want a good laugh? Learn to laugh at yourself. Do not take yourself too seriously. Remember to have fun. You will learn more if you do. What do you find funny about yourself? I think the way I walk and talk is sometimes funny. I find gender differences to be really funny. I think the way we misunderstand each other is funny and that some of our mistakes are funny. I think the way we dress is sometimes funny.

The root word of *functional* is fun. A fun relationship is the beginning of a functional home. As you will find, fun is a marker of how well we are meeting our relational intimacy needs. Without the need being met, we lose true fun. We lose joy. This is the first sign of burnout. Humor is the first to go. Humor can help bring us back to where He wants us. Find a way for both of you to have laughter. "All the days of the needy are bad, but a cheerful heart has a continual feast" (Proverbs 15:15) and Psalm 37:4, "Delight yourself in the Lord; and He will give you the desires of your heart."

Practice - Remember to Have Fun

- Draw a picture of yourself that exemplifies your humor style.
- Show the picture to your Same Page Partner and have them indicate how this represents you.
- How does it show your humor?
- How does it show your style?

Humor Check

Job 8:21 ESV, "He will yet fill your mouth with laughter, and your lips with shouting."

Comedy, joy, and laughter are good remedies. Look at the root word in *comedy* and *remedy*. The root is *med* from which we get the word *medicine*. Thus, we have co-med and re-med. Sounds like they mean the same thing to us, but co-med brings re-med just as we read in Proverbs 17:22, "A joyful heart is good medicine, but a broken spirit dries up the bones." Relational intimacy that is produced by comedy is a remedy.

There is also intimidating humor that brings despair and no remedy at all. Consider this to be a humor check. Does your humor bring a remedy to those who receive it? Is relational intimacy the result of your humor bringing people closer or does your sarcasm bring intimidation and push people away? You need to specifically ask others what is the result of your humor style in order to find out. This might not be easy if you don't like what you hear.

The Lord has a good deal to say about humor. The Word says that coarse jesting is not good, coarse jesting is humor that brings intimidation. Paul writes to the Ephesians, "There must be no filthiness or foolish talk, or vulgar joking, which are not fitting, but rather giving of thanks" (Ephesians 5:4). Elsewhere we read that laughter is good medicine. As we saw previously, that is the humor that will bring about relational intimacy.

Practice - Humor Check

Ask your Same Page Partner and five other people about your humor style. Write down what you heard.

- Write down five things they suggested you change.
- Write down two ways humor may result in relational intimacy.
- Write down two ways humor may lead to intimidation.

Humor with What's in a Name

"And you will be called by a new name which the mouth of the Lord will designate" (Isaiah 62:2).

The best way to compliment with an *i* is to say your Same Page Partner's name first, before the compliment. What is in a name? It is the identifier of the person. Do you remember being called names as a child? You could be hurt simply by someone calling you "fatty" or "grasshopper legs." We don't forget these insults because to be named something is powerful.

Consider the very first thing God did with Adam. Adams's first job as a human was to name the animals. Using names is a way to acknowledge and identify the person within.

You will also notice the best way to complement with an e is to know their names and the meaning or purpose in life they have. Then we come alongside them and help them fulfill their purpose in a different manner. A productive way to start out is to know the meaning of their name. Remember we are looking out the new belief window of intimacy in order to see ourselves as saints who sin yet are no longer sinners. We are saved by grace as a gift of God. That is our new name. Saint.

Practice - What's in a Name

Write down your first and middle name along with its definition. You may have to do some research on the meaning of the name.

1. First name
2. Middle name

Write down your Same Page Partner's first and middle namRe along with its definition. Again, you may need to do some research on the meaning of the name.

1. First name
2. Middle name

For the day, call them or write them by what their names mean. For example

1. Albert means bright nobility
2. James means leader

So, my partner would call me Bright Nobility Leader all day. You can see why I would like this task, as will you.

Pay Attention to the Humor

Is there a style or preference for humor in your life? In your partner's life? Pay attention to how your humor file is growing and hopefully, your use of humor is expanding. Have you been adding to it and sharing the humor with your Same Page Partner? Make a practice of sharing the humorous events in your life with your Same Page Partner. Have you told more funny stories than bad or wrong or sad stories? Laughter is medicine to the soul. It is better to use humor than to speak negative things. Commit to healthy humor at this time. A good rule of thumb is to pay attention to who is laughing during the humor. If both people aren't laughing, it probably isn't funny and your "humor" may be a cloak for an insult.

Practice - Pay Attention to the Humor

- Write down one thing you enjoy about laughing together with your Same Page Partner.
- Talk to your Same Page Partner about your use of humor and their use of humor, and what they resent and/or appreciate about both.

Chapter Six

Getting Through the Storms of Life Together

Anger Is a Response

People often ask me if God gets angry. The answer is yes, God gets angry. Does God sin? No. So that is how we ought to be. Anger can be a healthy expression of frustration or pain. We all feel angry. In fact, on average, researchers have found we get angry on average 250 times per day. If we can manage our expression of that anger, it can lead to healing and intimacy. Sin, however, is never healthy.

Relational intimacy with God, self, your Same Page Partner, and others means we will get angry at some point. We need to express that anger in healthy ways so that it drains from inside us. No insults allowed.

Practice - Anger Is a Response

This practice may not be easy for you. It might be the first time you have looked anger and resentment square in the eye. You may experience brain freeze or denial. Remain focused and diligent. Anger is one of the stages of grief. No need to stay stuck there to get through the storms of life.

Do this practice individually and then show the lists to your Same Page Partner. This task is called the Resent/Appreciate task of emotional breathing and has been the one task that couples have told me has helped them the most! Breathe out the old with the Resents and breathe in the new with the Appreciates.

- Write 10 "I resent" statements to include people, places, things or events and why they bother you. Example: I resent orange and white construction cones because they slow down traffic and that slows me down.
- Make a list of 20 "I appreciate" statements of people, yourself, places, things, or events you appreciate and why you appreciate them. Example: I appreciate all that the Lord has done for me because ...

Tips

The folks who developed this task were Gestalt psychologists back in the 60s. I heard them speak in the 70s and they stated that we have over 3,000 Appreciates in life. We have over 1,000 Resents in life that we carry each day. Yet, we talk about the Resents ten times more than the Appreciates. The Biblical examples in the Psalms use the term *lament* for Resents and *praise* for Appreciates. Every Psalm is either about a lament or a praise or both.

1. Did you remember to list some aspects of yourself as well?
2. Some aspects may show up on both lists. For example, you may appreciate orange and white construction barrels since they signify progress, fixing the road so it does not tear up your car. You may also resent orange and white barrels as they signify delays and detours.

3. Make this list second, as this exercise is a type of emotional breathing, breathing out the old resentments and breathing in the new appreciations. Does this sound familiar? You'll recognize Psalmists like David did this to word, song, and dance. Be creative.

Show both lists to your Same Page Partner.

Compare lists with your Same Page Partner and be extra creative. Be open and disclose in a kind way. Self-disclose without criticism. This practice is needed in all relationships. If you need help or a jumpstart, look at the Psalms or read the words of Jesus. They plainly make lists to help us to enjoy all that the Lord has for us. We can even learn to give thanks for everything in this way. Keep up the great work!

Understanding Compliments

It is time to practice complimenting each other in front of and to others so your Same Page Partner can learn to hear and accept it as truth. A genuine compliment is rooted in the truth so it has emotion involved. It is the opposite of flattery. The real compliment doesn't contain barbs of cynicism, intimidation, or criticism. A compliment builds up and encourages. Hebrews 3:13, "But encourage one another every day, as long as it is still called "today," so that none of you will be hardened by the deceitfulness of sin."

The media uses backward insults as part of the drama to support their ratings. The canned laughter after the barbed compliment is supposed to make us think it is funny. It isn't. It does not build up, it destroys.

Barbs hurt. They wound deeply at any age, but especially in children. Barbs intimidate and will block intimacy.

Another extreme is flattery. Flattery falls empty and is usually intended for the flatterer to get something and not to give something. Flattery sends a false message that I want you to think this is about you but it's really about me.

The Psalmist had strong opinions about flattery when he wrote, "For there is nothing trustworthy in their mouth; their inward part is destruction itself. Their throat is an open grave; they flatter with their tongue" (Psalms 5:9).

Compliments, however, give respect, honor, and value. Be a giver, complimenter, rather than a taker or an insulter.

Practice - Understanding Compliments

- Write down five sample compliments.

- Write down how to express those compliments in creative ways. For example, verbal, in writing, in art, or in gifts.

- Discuss your list of compliments with your Same Page Partner. What did you learn?

Learning to Compliment

"But in your hearts set Christ apart [as holy--acknowledging Him, giving Him first place in your lives] as Lord. Always be ready to give a [logical] defense to anyone who asks you to account for the hope and confident assurance [elicited by faith] that is within you, yet [do it] with gentleness and respect" (I Peter 3:15, AMP).

A vital component in relational intimacy, and worthy of repeating, is learning to give and receive compliments. The Bible is separated into more categories than simply the Old Testament and the New Testament. Psalms, Proverbs, and Song of Solomon, are a part of what is called Wisdom Literature. We compliment God all the time and probably don't even recognize that this is what we're doing. Praise and worship, at its core, is complimenting God the Father, Son, and Holy Spirit and The body of Christ, ourselves as the Church. Also consider the words of Jesus and the Apostles and their acts of gratitude and thanksgiving as forms of compliments.

Practice - Learning to Compliment

- Write 10 compliments to your Same Page Partner.
- Listen to your Same Page Partner's list and accept only by saying "thank you." It's important to remain positive and dismissing another person's view of you can be perceived as negative. This activity may feel awkward at first. We are not trained to receive compliments. They embarrass us. Sit through the discomfort. By diminishing or deflecting another person's compliment to us, we are denying them their own blessing. Joy comes to those who give and receive compliments.

Give compliments throughout the day, in many ways. If possible, try to compliment your Same Page Partner so other people will hear the compliment as well. In that way, many people are edified or built up in Christ. The opposite of compliment is to criticize. It is my opinion that there is no such thing as constructive criticism. Either there is constructive guidance or destructive criticism. One builds up and the other destroys. Be a life builder and give those compliments freely.

Four Modes for Finding Our Way

Paul's letter to the Ephesians can teach us so much about loving and caring for each other. "All bitterness, wrath, anger, clamor, and slander must be removed from you, along with all malice. Be kind to one another, compassionate, forgiving each other, just as God in Christ also has forgiven you" (4:31).

We have found that Scripture teaches that we are meant to act in one way. God's way. Jesus told us that He is the way the truth and light (John 14:6). So our journey would be easy, right? Just follow that one way and all will be well. But life isn't like that. It's complicated and we mess up all the time. Jesus' way is to do the right thing in the right spirit. But we often stray from this path. I have identified four modes explaining the one right way and the three wrong ways in which we can become lost.

List of Four Modes

1. We do the right thing in the right spirit.
2. We do the wrong thing in the wrong spirit.
3. We do the wrong thing in the right spirit.
4. We do the right thing in the wrong spirit.

We can find guidance for this in Paul's second letter to the Corinthians."Each one must do just as he has decided in his heart, not reluctantly or under compulsion, for God loves a cheerful giver" (9:7).

Here, Paul tells us to decide in our hearts what path to take which is easy enough when things are going well. But, the hardest time to do the right thing in the right spirit is when we are angry.

Anger Blocks Compliments

Anger will block our desire to compliment or receive compliments. It can eat them. Yes, anger can be expressed in the right way as stated throughout Scripture. We can follow the imperative, "Be angry yet do not sin, don't let the sun go down on your wrath." (Ephesians 4:26). James asks us to be slow to anger. There are plenty of Scriptures discussing anger and I encourage you to study them. Yet, to be like our Lord, we are to show forth His attributes. One attribute ascribed to Him over and over is that He is slow to anger. Even when He drove out the moneychangers, He only drove them out and declared the truth. He did not annihilate them as the law of the day called for. Yes, capital punishment was the penalty for what they were doing. Yet, He did not pass judgment at them; He displayed grace even in His anger. Overcoming anger to give and receive compliments is the practice to learn here.

Practice - Four Modes for Finding Our Way

- Write down your Same Page Partner's anger mode.
- Write down which mode your Same Page Partner gives to the Lord.
- Write down your Same Page Partner's fun mode.
- Write down a secret signal you both agree to that serves as a reminder to choose the appropriate mode when offering guiding opinions.

The Distinction Between Compliment and Complement

Complementing each other is different from complimenting each other. Complementing involves appreciating differences that make the relationship something more than can be imagined. Synergy is an outcome of a complementing that makes us more than we could be as an individual. The adages stronger together than apart, or, the sum of the parts is greater than each individual part help illustrate this idea. This does not mean, of course, that living a life alone is insufficient. I am saying that we cannot be all that we are meant to be unless we are relationally intimate and interdependent with others. We cannot do what we are called to do alone. We are nestled into a partnership with each other simply by living as humans. The neurotransmitter oxytocin is a stress hormone that prompts us to touch or hug another human to reduce stress. There are twelve times in the book of Hebrews that the term *Let us* is found to walk together in the way of Christ, our salvation is to be lived together.

Do not conflate complementing with harmony. Often, when we do things differently than each other, the relationship takes on a newness of life. A healthy, relationally intimate relationship must appreciate differences while respecting boundaries. Some of the ways to help others do look very different, while the way to eternal life is only one. Relational meaning comes as together we seek to do the same work in different ways. And the work is not limited to the relationship itself but rather all of the tasks and responsibilities we handle in a day. Most importantly, we are called to teach others about God. We do this by building relationships and modeling how our uniqueness is a gift from God. So embrace differences. Celebrate them. We need them to create ourselves as new in Christ.

The Body of Christ

When we ask, we receive answers. When we seek, we find. We knock and the door is opened to us. As a member of the fellowship of the Lord, we can accomplish things that we would be unable to do alone.

To stress this point, please do not think I am referring to singles or doubles (married). There is no one who is single in the Body of Christ. You may not be married, but you are not to be meant to feel alone, whether single or married. Your unique gifts and talents can complement many people, no matter your marital status. You can do things in a way no one else can do. You can appreciate the way you do things, and the way others do things. You can appreciate the outcome that is greater than what any of us can do alone.

Practice - the Distinction Between Compliment and Complement

- List several simple everyday tasks that you and your Same Page Partner do.
- List the ways you accomplish those tasks. For example, if you go make your coffee every morning, do you do so in pajamas in the dark?
- List the ways your Same Page Partner performs these tasks. For example, perhaps your partner is showered, fully dressed with music blaring when making the morning coffee.
- Consider ways in which you feel irritated by the way your partner performs the tasks differently from you.
- Consider ways you can accept and appreciate the way your partner's actions and choices differ from yours.

Jesus Is Our Overcomer So That We May Overcome

"You are from God, little children, and have overcome them; because greater is He who is in you than he who is in the world" (John 4:4).

Are you looking forward to your date? It will be a fun time together to celebrate the week you have had and a time to usher in the next week tomorrow with joy and laughter despite circumstances. God wants us to enjoy His healing in every area of life.

Practice - Jesus Is Our Overcomer So That We May Overcome
Write out the following verses over the next few days.

- Deuteronomy 30:19-20
- Psalms 91:9-10, 14, 16
- Proverbs 4:20-24
- Isaiah 53:4-5
- Mathew 15: 30-31
- Romans 8:2-11
- James 5: 14-16
- I Peter 2:24
- Nahum 1:9
- Psalms 118:17
- Tell your Same Page Partner what it is like reading the Bible together and enjoying being on the same page.

Chapter Seven

Money Principles

Money Causes Conflicts

$$$$$$$$$$$$$ "For the love of money is a root of all sorts of evil, and some by longing for it have wandered away from the faith and pierced themselves with many griefs" (I Timothy 6:10).

Money is not the root of all sorts of evil, but the love of money is. The way one handles money tells you a lot about myself. In many overlapping situations inside the relationship with your Same Page Partner, disclosing money matters is one way to build intimacy. But money issues are complicated. How we spend money or what we spend it on directly relates to our core beliefs and values. This can cause deep conflict within relationships when those values clash.

For example, one partner may have grown up in a family that went all out for Christmas. They bought the big tree and crammed it full of presents. There were feasts and treasures and activities. The money this family spent on Christmas was meant as an expression of love and family commitments. So when Christmas rolls around inside their relationship, they want to spend money as an expression of love. But what if their partner grew up in a home that celebrated Christmas by volunteering at a soup kitchen, perhaps they exchanged handmade gifts and enjoyed simpler pleasures to honor the holiday and each other. If the big celebration partner attempts to buy expensive gifts and decorations, his partner may see his actions as garish or even selfish. The way money is spent or not spent roots deeply into our childhoods. We are attached to money in emotional ways. This causes conflicts about extravagance or lack and even how to develop a shared definition of extravagance or lack.

Learning how to bridge these different belief systems around money will help you build a relationship rich with intimacy. Each partner must learn to balance their own views alongside the views of their partner. It is a learned skill that takes interdependent relationships to help us have the right attitude.

Practice - Money Causes Conflicts

- Write down your emotions surrounding your current financial situation.
- Read these feelings with your Same Page Partner.
- Write your earliest memory about money.
- Write two or three words describing your attitude around money.
- What power does money hold over you?
- Do you tend to save or spend money?
- Name a time you felt out of control when spending money.
- Name a time you felt in control when spending money.
- What are your thoughts on God's role with your money?
- Write down the dream gift you would give your Same Page Partner if money were not limited.

- Write down a meaningful gift you would give to your Same Page Partner that costs little or no money.

Think of the gifts brought to Jesus and the significance of each. Balanced views on money bring joy and intimacy that are not just significant, but vital.

Activity Checklist Two

1. Take a moment to write down where you are with money.
2. Make or buy your Same Page Partner a gift that discloses to them how you are about money.

Balancing Time and Money

Money check again. Is the saying true that time is money? I don't think so. Yet, how we choose to relate to time and how we relate to money tells us a lot about if our relational intimacy needs are being met. When relational intimacy needs are met, we greatly respect time and money. We do so in a caring and loving manner. We know that we are to love and serve the Lord, our God, with all that we have, including time and money.

When we are in a rigid, intimidating place in life, we will be rigid with time and money. Consider the idea that time and money are both things you spend. They are a valued commodity. It is interesting that if we clutch with clenched fists what little we have, our hands aren't open to receiving. Open hands of generosity, allow us to receive. Being with your Same Page Partner in the extreme of chaos is no fun and leaves others around us confused. We often lose friends because of time and money, especially when chaotic with both.

The Extinction Burst

It generally takes about three weeks to change a habit or stop a habit. In the three weeks, it takes to extinguish a habit, the urges to do the habit become stronger and while trying to extinguish it, the habit will intensify and increase. Hence, the extinction burst. our brain is made to resist change for survival and so we do not have to relearn everything every day. Whatever level the behavior is at when we apply an intervention, for the first week the behavior increases if we want it to decrease or decreases if we want it to increase. The first week is the hardest and the behavior, urges, and thoughts go in the opposite desired direction, so we generally think, *It's not working.*

Then we make a really big mistake. We stop the intervention and now we have conditioned ourselves to plateau in a worse place. The extinction burst is an expected phenomenon and shows the intervention is working! Do not stop the intervention!

Ever hear the adage "it gets worse before it gets better"? It's a true statement and based upon the extinction burst. An effective intervention produces an extinction burst where it gets worse before it gets better. What we want to increase decreases and what we want to decrease increases only for a short time and then the desired results are seen after a week of intervention.

That is the way it is supposed to be. We hold onto behaviors. Imagine if every morning we had to relearn all that we have learned?! Thank God for the extinction burst- even if dealing with a child or adult having a tantrum. Apply an effective intervention, and it will get worse before it gets better. If you stop the intervention too soon, you have just taught them to tantrum longer and louder. Hang on, just for a short time, and in due season you will see the desired results.

Remember the extinction burst – it is there with all behaviors of all ages.

Practice - The Extinction Burst

- List three habits you have around money.
- List three habits you have around time.
- Compare to your Same Page Partner's list and write down differences.

Usually in relationships, one is a saver and the other is a spender. Ask each other if your time and money habits reflect a balance in relational intimacy or if you are either rigid or chaotic, hoarding or excessive spending.

Relationship with Money

Money check. How is your relationship with money best described? Flaky? Rigid? Unknown Stranger? Is it your only friend? Trusted Companion? or Painful Problem? Really consider what money is or means to you. Expect your answer to be more than one thing. Ask your Intimate Other if they agree with your assessment. Would God agree with your call? His call, of course, is the one that matters. Ask Him what He thinks of how you relate to money. "Ask and it shall be given" (Matthew 7:7).

Much is said about money in the Scriptures. Mathew teaches that real treasure is stored in Heaven (6:21). Proverbs advises us to honor the Lord with our wealth (3:9). Paul advised Timothy that those who desire wealth may fall into temptation (6:9). Money is not a 21st-century invention. God has provided us with guidance about what money means and how to use it. He doesn't want us to be ignorant nor in worship of money. In the

Gospel records, Jesus spoke a great deal about money but not more than the Kingdom of God, which is righteousness, peace, and joy in the Holy Spirit (see Romans 14:17).

The key to the relationship with money is found in our questions about it. There are many teachings on how to balance a checkbook or how to keep your bank balance out of the red. But so, too, we must learn to have balanced ideas surrounding money and its use. How do we balance money? How do we hold money in balance? Do we own it, or does it own us? It's important to create a steady belief system around money. Confusion is not of God. Order is of God. Work to keep your relationship with money in order.

Luke wrote Jesus saying about money that, "No servant can serve two masters; for either he will hate the one and love the other, or he will be devoted to one and despise the other. You cannot serve God and wealth" (6:13).

Practice - Relationship with Money

- Write down an incident you found surprising about the way your Same Page Partner handled money.
- Read what you wrote down to your partner and listen to your partner's observations about you.
- Discuss with your partner.

Tithing

Money check. "Honor the Lord from your wealth and from the first of all you produce" (Proverbs 3:9).

Tithing 10% of our total gross income is challenging and exciting. When we tithe and give all that we have, to the Lord, we need to be cheerful, whether money, time, or talent. It might not be at first but continue doing so until the cheer comes along. If we consider all that God has given to us, the tithe will begin to feel quite small. The hardest time to tithe is when we are in debt, but that is the time we need to give so the most. Take care to learn if you are truly tithing on all your total gross income to the church you attend. If you are not attending a church, start looking for one to commit yourself to and then start giving or tithing there as the Lord leads.

Practice - Tithing

- Write down your thoughts on tithing.
- Share with your Same Page Partner and compare thoughts. Do so in a spirit of gentleness and openness.

Building Up Each Other as You Change

"Therefore, encourage one another and build one another up, just as you also are doing" (I Thessalonians 5:11). Change is very difficult and you need to encourage each other in the process of change, no matter what the area of change may be. Time to encourage each other in the journey thus far!

Practice - Building up Each Other as You Change

- Write down what you like about your Same Page Partner.
- Name something you find mysterious about your Same Page Partner
- Name three things you enjoy about spending time together-not what you enjoy but why you enjoy it.
- Fill in the blank.
- In our intimacy, I find ….
- Name two things that would change if your partner were not in your life.
- As you discuss these, repeat back to your Same Page Partner what you heard.

Chapter Eight

30-Minute Date

An Intimate Date

What time is it? Do you have time to do this? How much time will it take? Do we have enough time? Our lives are measured by and sometimes even ruled by time. Is time a friend or foe? The word *time* comes from Latin *tim* means *to relate* and the way we use it implies the relationship of the earth to the sun. The root word of intimate is *tim* or *time together* with the prefix *in* means *closely* or combined *to relate closely.* Intimate means to relate closely and that requires time with God, yourself, and your Same Page Partner.

In order to fulfill this lesson, you will need to set aside three-time frames to have three dates. The term date is tricky here in that it can mean a specific time and place or a romantic event. My use here overlaps both meanings depending on your relationship with your Same Page Partner.

Practice #1 - An Intimate Date

- Set a timer for 30 minutes. Write down thoughts concerning what it feels like to spend time with God. Remain focused with no distractions.

- Set a timer for 30 minutes. Write down thoughts concerning what it feels like to spend time with yourself. Remain focused with no distractions.

- Set a timer for 30 minutes. Write down thoughts concerning what it feels like to spend time with your Same Page Partner. Remain focused with no distractions.

Remember to have fun. Silly may or may not be ok in your relationship, but do have fun.

Practice #2 - An Intimate Date

Go on a date with your Same Page Partner. Do something atypical for you and make certain it is within your agreed budget. A big part of this task is that there must be no interruptions. That's right. It will feel odd, at first, to leave your phone on off or to turn off the television. But this time is sacred and devoted to one purpose. Allow nothing to disturb you. This time is precious and to reach relational intimacy, it must be guarded. If something goes wrong or doesn't start out right, relax. You are making an important beginning in a memory that will last a long time.

What Is a Date?

God enjoyed time with Adam and Eve communing in the Garden (see Genesis 2-3). He walked with them in the quiet of the day. They enjoyed perfect communion with God, self, and each other.

Think of dates as something meant to be kept and not broken.

What is a date? It starts with an actual date, a day on the calendar for a time and place of togetherness. It becomes an expression of relational intimacy that occurs and builds a deeper bonding. Alone together and together alone. Yet, not ever alone because relational intimacy excludes aloneness. We do not like to be alone because God said that it is not good for us to be alone. That is a declaration of truth.

Sometimes we can go on a date and feel alone. We may believe the other person doesn't understand us. Maybe they don't hold our attention. When we feel alone, a date is a cure to prove to ourselves that we are not alone. Genesis 1:31, "And God saw all that He had made, and behold it was very good." If somehow, you feel alone on a date, then open yourself up to being vulnerable. Dare to risk telling your date how you are feeling. Let the disclosure begin. Talk about loneliness and what you view as the source. Loneliness in marriage is a greater pain than loneliness in being single many would say. The truth is that loneliness has nothing to do with relationship status. It has to do with if your relational intimacy need is being met. It is an indicator of what you are feeling intimately and deeply. People can feel lonely in a crowd, for example. Talk about the point of relational intimacy that you feel is missing. Please talk. Just keep talking. You will find your way.

In Paul's letter to the Ephesians, he discusses how to speak the truth, saying, "But speaking the truth in love, we are to grow up in all aspects into Him who is the head, that is, Christ" (4:15). When Pauls writes, "Grow up in all aspects into Him" he could mean for us to grow in intimacy as well.

Practice #3 - An Intimate Date

Get ready to go on another date. But this one needs to be one whereby you can write and listen. You are going to practice active listening skills. Think about what you are hearing and stay focused. Do not prepare a rebuttal in your head. Stay in the moment. Listen. Oh yeah, lighten up and use humor to enjoy being on the same page with your partner. Review the activities in Chapter 1 prior to the date.

- Write down what you like about how your partner looks tonight.
- Ask your partner to tell a secret then write down what you heard her say.
- Compare your interpretation to her actual meaning.

Ebbs and Flows of a Relationship

The Groom: You who sit in the gardens: My companions are listening for your voice let me hear it.

The Bride   Hurry, my beloved, and be like a gazelle or a young stag on the mountains of balsam trees (Song of Solomon 8:13-14).

What is a date? You know, a real date. It can be a thrilling time of togetherness. A time of anticipation. A time. A great time. Time. Time with and time away. With each other and away from all else. There in body, soul, and spirit. Totally there for each other. Connecting in a wonderful way. You can feel exhilarated in meeting expectations.

After a while, a date can feel routined or entrenched. The routine captures the thrill. The routine becomes a rut. Nothing happens. Disconnection occurs. Distractions enter. Relational chaos sets in. The discomfort level will rise enough that you must confront the truth. Or, as a colleague of mine says, "carefront the truth." Show you care by talking about the issues, discuss together who is feeling what. Make certain to not assume that your partner feels the same way you do. Leave them space to speak their own experience of the truth. Examine your patterns as dating partners. Does drudgery follow excitement all the time?

Be comforted in the ebb and flow of all relationships. Seasons are to be expected in our dates. Our efforts to enjoy are to be gauged upon the season we are in. The season of the relationship determines the type of effort we put forth. In the winter season of the relationship, work at keeping the embers glowing. In spring, enjoy the exhilarating feeling of life. In summer, kick back and enjoy the lazy times together. In the fall, prepare for the relationship with hard work. Solomon is the accepted author of Ecclesiastes and is considered a wise man by God. He said, "There is an appointed time for everything, and there is a time for every matter under the sun" (3:1). Allow your relationship to expand and contract within its seasons.

Practice - Ebbs and Flows of a Relationship
    Consider the relational seasons in the discussion.
    Spring: time for refreshing, airing out, and rejuvenation.
    Summer: time for fun, relaxation, and playtime.
    Fall: time for hard, preparational and foundational work.
    Winter: time for steady, reliable warmth.
    Fill in the table in the Workbook.

Be Thankful

"Be filled with the Spirit… always giving thanks for all things in the name of our Lord Jesus Christ to our God and Father" (Ephesian 5:15).

On this day, we will return to thanksgiving for being able to enjoy being on the same page with our partner. Be thankful.

Choose to be thankful. Choose to see all the things the Lord has done for you. The road to ruin *begins* with unthankfulness and ingratitude (see Romans 1). Both appreciation and affirmation are the key to rich and lively relationships. Jesus wants us to choose to be thankful in life and for life. Thankfulness is the prerequisite to deep, lasting relationships. It is like the fuel that makes a jet soar. Without fuel, we cannot soar. fuel, no soar. Or to put it another way; no fuel, we feel sore. Prayer without thankfulness in all things is sore. Prayer with thankfulness makes us soar together in our relationships.

Mounting up with wings as eagles requires an attitude of gratitude. Where there is ingratitude, we crash and burn. Been there, done that. Even the little annoyances in our lives are placed there so we can be grateful for all things. Whining, grumbling and complaining bring about wandering "And all the sons of Israel grumbled against Moses and Aaron; and the entire congregation said to them, 'If only we had died in the land of Egypt. Or even if we had died in this wilderness'" (Numbers 14:2). Grumbling makes us wander like the Israelites in their journey in the desert. A three week walk took 40 years because of grumbling. Our relational needs will go unmet when we grumble and we will miss out on righteousness, peace, and joy. Thankfulness makes us soar in the Kingdom of God.

Practice - Be Thankful

- Make a list of 10 things you appreciate about the Lord.
- Make a list of 10 things you appreciate about yourself.
- Make a list of 10 things you appreciate about your Same Page Partner.

Process of the Four Stages

The stages of relational development are forming, norming, storming, and then performing your mission in life. "Mission Possible" as Tim Tebow calls it. Some relationships do not get past storming. They shipwreck or divorce (split-apart) adjourn during the storm. Or, they get past one storm and think that is all they will ever have. Each new event in life can bring opportunities for storming. Each addition to the household whether two-legged or four-legged, means we start all over again with forming, norming, storming, and performing. We go through this process many, many times in a relationship with God, self, or others. Get through the storm and the performance will follow.

Activity - Process of the Four Stages

Go on a conflict-free outing. The whole time you are together, promise each other not to conflict about anything for the entire duration. Conflict is a part of life and helps us to grow, but conflict need not be 24/7. Carve out a time to avoid conflict and instead, truly, deeply enjoy each other. Conflict resolution skills are good to know for the occasional conflict that arises. However, for the time of this outing with you and your Same Page Partner, no conflict. Before your outing physically or intellectually put your conflicts in a basket that must remain at home. This exercise is not the time for practicing conflict resolution. This is the time to have fun.

Tell each other about what it is like performing together on the same page. It truly becomes a concert of harmony.

Review of Biblical Meditation

"Come close to God and He will come close to you" (James 4:8).

In our A.C.T.S. M.E. acronym to help us to be intimate with our Creator, the fifth type of prayer to draw us close is M for meditation. Biblical meditation is dwelling upon God and who He is and what He has done. Biblical meditation is the opposite of worldly meditation that empties our thoughts and thinks upon ourselves.

We are to meditate upon God's Word, the Bible, and empty ourself of sin and shame, and then think upon God and who He has made us to be. The more we meditate upon Him and His work, the more we understand Him and can become more like Him.

Activity - Review of Biblical Meditation

- Ask God to show you three life Scriptures passages that you found earlier, to give you direction and reveal His purpose in creating you. These will be verses in the Bible that resonate His Truth in you and for you. As you move through the Bible, these verses may appear to jump out at you when you've read them.
- Write down the three life Scriptures.
- Share those life Scriptures with your Same Page Partner. Tell them about the purpose and joy you experience when meditating in the Bible.

Mirroring God's Relationship with Himself

"More than that, I count all things to be loss in view of the surpassing value of knowing Christ Jesus my Lord, for whom I have suffered the loss of all things, and count them mere rubbish, so that I may gain Christ" (Philippians 3:8).

Is my relationship with me a reflection of God's relationship within Himself? That's a hard question. Ouch. Stop the pain of that one. Does God ask painful questions? Yes, and only for our own good in finding relational intimacy with God, ourselves, and others. Just ask Job and see the questions he asked God and how God answered.

Growing pains are good pains. Growing pains are God's pains. The pains in my story have equipped me to bring joy to others in counseling them and in writing this book. Lamenting these pains is biblically sound when we eventually turn from lament to joy as seen in the book of Job, the oldest book in the Bible. Complaining about these facts is not what God would have us do. Psalms of Lament are a genre in the Book of Psalms, that expresses the hurt while still putting trust in God. Lament is followed by praise. The Lord turns a spirit of heaviness into a garment of praise! Complaining is the same as saying God made a mistake thus, not trusting Him. Lamenting is saying this hurts but I am trusting in the Lord through it all! It is the healthy fear of God that says we don't want to ever say God makes a mistake. Believe Him at His Word. He does not make mistakes. He does work all things for good. Romans 8:28 "And we know that God causes all things to work together for good to those who love God, to those who are called according to *His* purpose."

Practice - Mirroring God's Relationship with Himself

- Review the first chapter of this book. Ask yourself how your relationship with yourself reflects God's relationship with Himself.
- List five ways in which it does. Remember this is His purpose for us as seen in the verse above, Romans 8:28.
- List five ways in which it doesn't.
- Share your lists with your Same Page Partner.

Chapter Nine

The Four Faces of Jesus

"As for the form of their faces, each had a human face; all four had the face of a lion on the right and the face of a bull on the left, and all four had the face of an eagle" (Ezekiel 1:10).

In this passage, Jesus the Messiah, was prophetically described as having four faces.

Parallel to that prophetic passage is the prophetic passage of Apostle John in Revelation 4:7, where the creatures reflect Christ as they are in His presence and reflect Him. "The first living creature was like a lion, the second creature like a calf, the third creature had a face like that of a man, and the fourth creature was like a flying eagle."

Prophecies are rarely straightforward and are often presented through imagery. Because interpretation can be subjective, scholars present a myriad of views. Some interpret the four faces to coincide with the four Gospels in the New Testament as you will see as you read on. One of the four faces is emphasized in each Gospel though not at the exclusion of the other three faces.

Each of the four faces can represent a style of interaction. To be like Jesus, we must seek direction from Him, the Father, and the Spirit about what face to present in any situation, at any time in a relationship. Let's examine each face to understand its characteristics.

Understanding the Lion Face

The lion's face is authoritative and commanding. In Numbers, the author writes, "The lion raises itself; it will not lie down until it devours the prey and drinks the blood of those slain" (23:24). This is a violent image, yes, but consider the strength and authority imagined here. Samuel is full of lion references in regards to David. Standing in front of Goliath, he is unafraid because he feels he has overcome stronger adversaries. "And David said, 'The Lord who saved me from the paw of the lion and the paw of the bear, He will save me from the hand of this Philistine'" (I Samuel 17:37). David's fearlessness in front of a giant, stems from his bravery in besting the lion. David himself had a lion's heart. When we face danger or feel afraid, this is the time to use the face of the lion.

In addition to fierceness, the lion can also mean royalty. C. S. Lewis, in his trilogy, *The Lion, the Witch and the Wardrobe* forever imbued our image of God as royal and refined, as seen through Aslin. But there are biblical references as early as the prophet Amos, saying, "A lion has roared, who will not hear? The Lord God has spoken" (3:8).

The Gospel of Matthew emphasizes that face. The lion rules and has dominion. The lion sets boundaries and gives directives. The lion is royalty. Jesus is the lion of the tribe of Judah. The Gospel of Matthew begins with a genealogy of Jesus to show that truth. We are worshippers in the house of David on the Mount of Zion. We can then obey the commandments given on the Mount of Sinai.

As we enter into His praise, we compliment the Lord for His glory and all He has given us. We then can love the Lord our God with all our heart, mind, soul, and strength. And then we will fulfill His commission to love our neighbors as ourselves and to make disciples of all the nations - both commands issued in the Gospel of Matthew and throughout His Word. We must wear the face of the lion when we need to remember our status as heirs of the King.

Practice - Understanding the Lion Face

- List three things you find difficult in drawing close to God the Father, God the Son, and God the Holy Spirit.
- List three barriers you create that interfere with intimacy with God the Father, God the Son, and God the Holy Spirit.
- Discuss with your Same Page Partner.

Understanding the Ox Face

The ox serves. The oxen work together in teams. The oxen do not make a lot of noise when they work. That is why the phrase we sing, "the cattle are lowing…" is significant in that the only noise oxen ever makes is so low that it is called "lowing." Consider this when wearing the face of the ox. It is a quiet thing, introspective and uncontentious.

The ox face does not demand recognition or position. The ox face is the face we are to wear when we serve God and others. Consider these verses, "Serve Him with gladness and enter His courts with thanksgiving" (Psalms 100:4). "Choose this day whom you will serve" (Joshua 24:15). "Before us each day is set life and death, which will we serve" (Deuteronomy 30:19).

Will we advocate justice for the poor, the needy, and the oppressed or will we selfishly pursue our own wants? The ox face helps us to choose servanthood. When an ox comes to a fork in the road, it only goes in the direction it is led. The ox face always submits to the will of God, never its own.

When we think of an ox, we think of a beast of burden. Hard-working, obedient and useful. But an ox was often used in sacrifice to God. "Just as it is removed from the ox of the sacrifice of peace offerings); and the priest is to offer them up in smoke on the altar of burnt offering" (Leviticus 4:10). So, the animal was considered significant enough to please God. And God was particular about what kind of ox. He wanted only the finest. Deuteronomy says, "You shall not sacrifice to the Lord your God an ox or a sheep which has a blemish or any defect, for that is a detestable thing to the Lord your God" (17:1). So God saw oxen both as pragmatic and worthy.

Wear the ox face when you require discipline and grit to accomplish something difficult or dulling. But while in the trenches of servanthood, remember that your sacrifice is pleasing to God.

Practice - Understanding the Ox Face
- List three things you could do to serve the difficult people in your life.
- Share this list and discuss how you would feel serving them with your Same Page Partner.

Understanding the Man Face

We all know that man was born into sin and redeemed through Jesus' death. Often, Christians consider humanity to be flawed and needing to be fixed. We ask God for grace to overcome our weaknesses. But it's important to note that Jesus referred to Himself as man, and He was flawless. Mathew says, "But so that you may know that the Son of Man has authority on earth to forgive sin. Then He said to the paralyzed man, 'Get up, pick up your stretcher and go home.'" (9:6). So perhaps wearing the man face can mean more than fallibility and emotion.

Later in Matthew, he writes, "Just as the Son of Man did not come to be served, but to serve, and to give His life as a ransom for many" (20:28). This gives us a glimpse of when to wear the man face. When we are tending to others and sacrificing ourselves for the glory of God through service, do so in celebration of your own humanity.

The man face of Jesus is our emphasis at this time. Being human is what God chose for us. This was His sovereign plan. Jeremiah wrote, "Before I formed you in the womb, I knew you. And before you were born, I consecrated you" (1:5). He desires us to be the humans He intended when He created us. The Gospel of Luke emphasizes the human face of Jesus. He writes that Jesus was real with people. Most people liked being around Him. Despite his deity, He did not have an air of superiority. For us, the process of being human is to admit strengths and weaknesses exist side by side. Above all creatures, we have the ability to display a range of emotions. Anger, joy, laughter, tears? These are unique to the human condition. So the man face is one of tempered emotion and cognition. He created us for His good pleasure. "Everyone who is called by my name and whom I have created for my glory, whom I have formed, even whom I have made" (Isaiah 43:7). We find pleasure in giving Him pleasure. We can then extend that glory into our intimate relationships.

Practice - Understanding the Man Face

- Make a list who you are, or who you are meant to be in Christ (not actions).
- Restate tha as I am statements.

Understanding the Flying Eagle Face

The flying eagle face typifies being spiritual in prayer and fasting and soaring above problems to gain perspective. The adage *birds eye view* can be applied to the flying eagle face. Sometimes we need distance to gain perspective. We often hyper-focus on one problem and fail to see how it is connected to a larger, less complicated picture. Wearing the eagle face can remind us to back up for a minute and take in the whole landscape.

But the eagle is also a bird of majesty. Watch the eagle fly with reverential awe. Isaiah wrote, "Yet those who wait for the Lord will gain new strength; they will mount up with wings like eagles, they will run and not get tired, they will walk and not become weary" (40:31). So the image of an eagle here represents restoration and strength.

We see this beautifully said and foretold in Revelation "They will see His face, and His name will be on their foreheads" (22:4). I strongly encourage you and your Same Page Partner to read the entire chapter.

There are faces Jesus never wore. The rat face, the chicken face, the ostrich face, the skunk face, the snake face, and the turkey face, to name a few, were never ones He wore, and again neither should we. Think of a few more we are not to wear. Prayer and fasting are the hallmark behaviors of the flying eagle. In John's book of Revelation where the flying eagle face of Jesus is emphasize. In the Gospel of John. Like Daniel, we are to pray and fast both with regularity and spontaneity. He is closer to the Father in the Spirit as He prays and fasts. Daniel 9:3, "So I gave my attention to the Lord God, to seek *Him by* prayer and pleading, fasting, sackcloth, and ashes." Yes Jesus was accessible to the disciples. The high priestly prayer of John 17 is worth reading again and again. The hope He gives us in that prayer is to see what He wants for us to soar in victory and since He wants it, it will happen. His Word is always fulfilled. His Word is always fulfilled in us. The imagery of the flying eagle, indeed and of all four faces evokes us to a unity with Him and with each other that is righteousness, peace, and joy in the Holy Spirit.

Practice - Understanding The Flying Eagle Face
- With your Same Page Partner, list 10 people to pray for.
- Pray for them with your Same Page Partner.
- List ten needs you have in your life.
- Pray for them with your Same Page Partner.
- Step back and watch good things happen.

Balancing the Four Faces

Can you see that if only one of these faces is ever worn, problems occur? For example, the lion face alone is dictatorial, the ox face alone leads to burnout, the man face alone is simply good or not so good, and the flying eagle face alone is too heavenly-minded to be useful in any earthly way. Jesus is an equal balance of the four. So, we too, like Jesus are to be four-faced as He leads. With discernment, we can learn which experience requires which face to wear in the situation but be cautious to not rely on the one that feels the most familiar. We are meant to be multifaceted in Christ. Wear each face with equal enthusiasm.

Practice - Balancing the Four Faces
- Name one area in your life where you chose to go your own way and not God's way.

- Name a group of people or a person who you have a difficult time relating to.
- List five ways to begin to serve that group or person.
- Discuss with your Same Page Partner with lowing or gentle speech.

Chapter Ten

Time for Healing

Anxiety and Depression are Fruits, not Roots

Anxiety and depression are the symptoms of something wrong. They are the indicator lights on the dashboard that something is not right with the engine, fuel, systems, or tires.

What is it that is not right? My belief is that the relational intimacy need is not met. If someone is panicking from choking or drowning, it is because another basic need is not met – air. Depression and anxiety are there as we struggle in panic for the relational intimacy need to be met. Songwriters compare love and relational intimacy to air, water, or food.

Relational intimacy is our number one need above air, water, food, and sleep. When the need for relational intimacy goes unmet, our spirit, soul, and body go into panic mode with anxiety and depression manifesting. Meet the need for relational intimacy, and the anxiety and depression will subside along with the panic. Of course, the chronic stress from the need unmet for so long may make recovery more difficult. And if we medicate the chronic stress, with addictions, recovery will be more difficult as well.

First things first, meet the need!

Where Does Healing Begin?

Where to begin? Connect with your Creator. You are not a random accident. You are a planned gift from the Creator, who wants to be close to you. You determine how close. I recommend very close. The Creator, I believe, is the triune Father, Son, and Holy Spirit. You can relate to each Person of the Trinity in spending time complimenting, complementing, and enjoying the mystery as unfolding. Relating to our Creator is the most mysterious adventure one can imagine. The depth of meaning that ensues is multifaceted and not static. It is dynamic and pleasant. Any thoughts otherwise are from old patterns of thinking that are not true.

New beliefs are required to experience joy in the place of anxiety and depression. But you will feel immeasurable joy in place of anxiety and depression when the relational intimacy need is met with God, self, and others.

Next, intimacy with self. Journaling is a tool to assist you in this endeavor. Writing down the old emotions experienced and the new emotions you want to feel are most important. What new thoughts do you want to think, and what old thoughts do you want to jettison? Journaling these areas daily for three weeks will assist you greatly.

Practice - Where Does Healing Begin?

- Fill in the table in your Workbook to begin the path to relational intimacy. We probably have over a thousand people, places, and things, we resent and over three thousand appreciates according to Gestalt researchers. Just hit the high points.

- Build an intimacy circle with five to seven others with whom you could share anything and everything about yourself without fear of reprisal. Jesus had six people in His inner circle, three men, Peter, James, and John, and three women, Mary, her sister Martha, and Mary Magdalene. Relational intimacy with God, self, and others will propel you in joy in life. All the old beliefs and fears are simply not true. God is a good Father who wants His kids to have joy, and to know they are wanted, planned, and loved more than they can imagine.

God Already Knows

Our Lord's Kingdom brings righteousness, peace, and joy in the Holy Spirit. His healing freely brings gifts into our lives. It is time for the things of the kingdom of darkness to leave. Hidden in the basement of our souls are contempt, shame, and despair. We have hidden away the things that we do not want anyone else to know. Now is the time to clean out our basements and fill them with light. It is only in this work that our darkness can be healed through our Savior and Friend, Jesus Christ, our Lord. There is no need to be shy here. Whatever it is, He already knows it, and He wants to bring healing from it. As long as our secrets remain hidden in the basement of our souls, they will bring agony and cyclical defeat.

But, when we choose to reveal our sins to the light, and we deal with them, we have victory over defeat. We go from victim to victor. But victory is beyond resilience and beyond grit, if we go it alone. Partnered with God, we can overcome our weaknesses which then serve as testimony in bringing hope to others to set them free from their prisons.

We must learn to no longer look out the old belief window but rather to look out the new belief window. We are new creatures in Christ. Paul wrote in his letter to the Corinthians, "Therefore if anyone is in Christ, this person is a new creation; the old things passed away; behold, new things have come" (5:17).

Differences Between Shame and Anxiety

Anxiety can be meaningful in small doses. Reducing it to a small dose in our life is the key to joy. Joy and anxiety cannot coexist in a person, but anxiety can let the person know that something is not right. As we seek to fill our relational intimacy need, joy will emerge when the need is filled.

External circumstances cannot undermine the state of joy. Happiness is fleeting, so anxiety can disrupt happiness. Joy is a state of being that anxiety cannot disrupt. Anxiety is like a dashboard light indicating a problem. Happiness does not fix the problem. Relational intimacy with God, self, and others fixes the problem, and the state of joy permeates one's being. Worries dissipate, stress becomes manageable, and negative self-talk is silenced. Joy fills one's being, and a state of contentment follows.

The Apostle Paul writes to the Philippians, "I know what it is to be in need, and I know what it is to have plenty. I have learned the secret of being content in any and every situation, whether well fed or hungry, whether living in plenty or in want. I can do all this through him who gives me strength" (4:12-13).

Finding other core reasons for the anxiety in each individual can assist in keeping the anxiety under control. Awareness is half the battle. Journaling when the anxiety increases and subsides can provide clues for the core reasons. Shame can increase anxiety, but guilt does not. Guilt is knowing *I did something wrong* and can admit it. Shame is *I am wrong, a mistake, and I'm no good.* This is a false belief we carry from five years old to the end of believing that belief.

Anxiety and shame do go hand in hand as toxic intimidation to our being. Intimate means to relate closely, while intimidate means to remove close relating. Intimidation is anything that works against us in filling the need of relational intimacy. Making our relationships and our workplaces/homes a No Shame Zone is something to strive for. One way to do that is to call out intimidating behaviors for what they are. Intimacy killers. Enhance intimacy behaviors, so they thrive wherever you are. Choose to choose joy for your reaction to difficult situations and people. Give more compliments than criticisms. Give correction with joy and no shame.

Choosing Joy to Break the Shame Addiction

Shame is addicting, and it kills. Suicide is often fueled by shame. Suicide is a way to divorce oneself instead of forgiving oneself. Jesus came to earth to die a horrific death, to forgive our sins, and remove the shame we bear. He was raised from the dead and lives seated at the right hand of the Father. We can be free from shame unless we are addicted to it, and we hold on to it.

Shame is the ultimate *I'm no good*. Shame keeps us from liking ourselves and being relationally intimate with ourselves. Healthy *me time* is often disrupted by thoughts of inadequacy and insecurity, with flashback memories of those events as intrusive thoughts. Then random thoughts of impending doom follow due to negative experiences and adverse experiences, and a flood of shame washes over us. We learn to like it and get addicted to it at a young age.

Those of us who have been sexually abused think our future is ruined since we lost our virginity at age three, or twelve, or whatever age. The sexual abuse puts us on a trajectory to despise our self and self-loathing with contempt of self sets in. Divorcing ourselves sounds appealing, and that results in suicide.

The shame restrains us from reaching out for help. We think no one will understand when thousands of us do understand and have had the same thoughts and feelings from the same childhood events. Fentanyl, oxycontin, and heroin, and other drugs that to try to stop the thoughts and divorce the self are consumed like candy in our neighborhoods because the prevalence of childhood sexual abuse and other adverse childhood experiences.

Please embrace the very thing you are running from. Be relationally intimate with God, self, and others. Being relationally intimate with Jesus is the place to start. He died to remove the effects of the sins against you and the shame that has scarred you. It is a process and usually not an instant removal of shame and harm. Live one day at a time and choose joy in life while rising from victim to victor in resilience. Reach out for support and embrace those around you to help you. Many of us can relate to and assist you. There is hope in Christ; there is always hope! Hope is found in meeting our relational intimacy need.

Hope breaks the addiction to shame, and joy follows to keep the shame away. Choosing joy each day is a value at Rock Hills Church. Being reminded to do so helps. Feel the joy of living each day. The past does not have to keep you from joy today. Joy is a gift for you for today, no matter what has happened in the past. No matter how much you remember from the past, Jesus set you free. Receive the gift of joy and choose joy!

Plato's Cave Analogy

Much like our reaction to walking out of a dark cave into the bright light of day, the transformation in Christ unfolds, and beauty rises from the ashes. Plato discussed this phenomenon in his Cave Analogy. A man sat inside a cave facing the wall, which projected images from the shadows behind him. If a person built a fire outside the mouth of the cave, for example, the man inside would see this displayed on his wall. As long as he sat inside the cave, he believed the images to be real. He didn't understand that they simply represented something real. Until he turned around and looked into the light, he was unaware that he was experiencing only a facsimile of real life. A copy. Only until we choose to walk out of the cave of false images can we glory in the light of the Lord.

Joy replaces mourning. Isaiah said we will be given, "The cloak of praise instead of a disheartened spirit" (61:3). Many of our hidden darknesses were stashed in the basements of our lives during early childhood. So what happened at an age before twelve years old now can trigger defensive and sometimes self-destructive behaviors within you as an adult. This means that now, a trigger or anniversary of a negative event or memory causes you to react in unhealthy or ungodly ways. These actions, performed in a kind of unresolved trauma zone, then spark the shame cycle. Shame is magnified, and our despair heightens.

Childhood Traumas

Think about how if, as an adult, you were in a car accident and how many people you would tell about the trauma of that event. More than likely, you would talk to a number of people about it. Think of the healing from the trauma that would come as you talked about it.

Now think about being a child, and something so bad happened to you that you can't even believe it happened. The intense shame of the event would keep you silent about it. Consider the abject fear and loathing of yourself from the event that you would experience. Think of the damage and harm that would have on the child into adulthood. One does not simply shake it off or bounce back.

Healing of silent secrets is a long and winding road that becomes better only as one learns to be relationally intimate with God, self, and others, even about the event. The shame melts away. The self-loathing turns to *I like me*. The victim becomes the victor. Healing occurs, and usually, the healed one becomes a healer of others with the same silent secret. Victim to victor becomes a healer for other victims, moving them from victim to victor. Regeneration in Christ Jesus produces regeneration and joy in life is restored as the Lord restores what the locusts have eaten.

Joel 2:25

"Then I will compensate you for the years

That the swarming locust has eaten,

The creeping locust, the stripping locust, and the gnawing locust—

My great army which I sent among you."

In this prophetic metaphor, the Lord is saying that even though He allowed the events that brought us pain and suffering, He will redeem them and compensate us with glory beyond our comprehension.

There is joy in the morning, beauty from ashes, and praise from heaviness. Serenity and acceptance with forgiveness are so beautiful. Wisdom is so wondrous to behold. Indescribable joy follows the storms that so easily beset us in the old ways, the old days. But now, in the new ways, the new days, things are different and much better. Stepping back and viewing life through a new lens is so much better. But it took time and work and a willingness to do things differently to do things in a new way. Meeting our relational intimacy need.

Congratulations. Celebrate!

Chapter Eleven

My Story

My Own Childhood Trauma

Between the ages of two and three, I had six surgeries to save my life. But these surgeries had a negative by-product. They traumatized me beyond imagination. For those of you in the psychotherapy, counseling, or mental health fields, you will understand what it means to say that those events sent my Adverse Childhood Experiences score off the charts. I had to wear painful apparatuses to recover from the surgeries. The Centers of Disease Control says that adverse childhood experiences (ACEs) can tremendously impact future violence, victimization, and perpetration. Unresolved, they can cause adverse effects on health and opportunities. And ACEs can affect you for the entire course of your life. ACEs are why it's so important to drag these terrors and memories out of the scary basement and face them in God's bright, safe light.

I suffered from undescended testicles. This condition is not all that rare; one in twenty-five boys is born this way. But in 1957 and 1958, when I required treatment, the surgeries were nearly barbaric. Today, the treatment is nearly outpatient with laser procedures. But in my time, a double hernia operation required that I wear a metal apparatus so the area could heal. Today, this type of harness would be cruel and unusual. But it was the standard practice at the time. My body treated my undescended testes as an infection. They were not where they belonged, so my body fought against them.

I have a profound memory of myself in a small room in the hospital. I was isolated due to the possibility of an infection, but the room felt hostile and punitive with the metal woven through the protective window panes. I remember screaming in pain and seeing my parents through that meshed safety glass. They were both crying and holding each other, likely feeling helpless to comfort me. I was isolated and separated from everyone in what felt like a sterile jail cell. Unable to reach each other, we endured our pain with no solace.

Even though these surgeries were life-saving, they put me on a trajectory of despair. This trauma affected my life in ways I could not have imagined from that hospital bed. Every two years from the anniversary of a marriage, a new job, or any life event makes me want to change or self-destruct.

The surgeries rendered me sterile because the trauma centered around my sexual organs. My body registered the events as sexual abuse trauma. It would take me decades to find healing within the Lord, and eventually, I could use my former basement-dwelling pain to guide others to healing.

But the journey from darkness to light was a protracted one. I was incessantly preoccupied with sex which later manifested as sex addiction. The immense shame I carried was more than I could handle. The shame then sent me to alcohol and drugs to smooth the rough edges of my pain. I self-medicated early in my childhood and through my teens and twenties. I didn't fully address my drug and alcohol addiction until I was 29, even though I was working in mental health during those years!

A New Life

On October 29, 1985, at 29 years old, a month before my 30th birthday, the Lord delivered me. I was crying out to Him to deliver me from the intense pain I was in following the suicide of two people I knew and cared for, for being away from God, and for my unmet relational intimacy needs!

During my third time in rehab, the doctors decided to treat the childhood traumas. There were other times of sexual abuse and physical abuse.

When I was three years old, the doctors told my parents to give me rum to help me sleep and not be "rambunctious." In the late 1950s, it was not uncommon for doctors to tell parents to administer rum to calm children in medical distress. So, my parents, following the orders of my pediatrician, served me rum as a medicinal remedy to my distress. And oh, how I learned to love rum. Children are clever at getting what they want, and I was no exception. I quickly learned ways to get more rum from my parents. Upon discharge from that third time in rehab on October 1, 1985, at 29 years old, I have been clean and sober since then.

Then, there was addiction to food. Being Italian-American, when I would come home from school, my mom would ask how my day was, and if I said good, I got a plate of spaghetti. If I said bad, it was a plate of lasagna. So, I had a lot of bad days. Remember, whatever we learn in the first 12 years of life is the hardest to change.

But, along with my alcohol addiction, my preoccupation with sex and the shame that followed continued into my adult life. It was so bad and so unresolved that when I would attempt sexual intimacy, images of those surgeries and recovery, as well as times of abuse, would trespass into my head with vivid recollections.

I have a vivid, accurate memory and it got so bad that I finally stopped having sex. That is not good for a marriage. I have plenty of physical scars from several surgeries. I still have the entropic re-enactment that happens every two to three years where I want to bolt. His light has brought healing to these tendencies. And, I am aware and equipped, so when I am tempted to fall back into the old coping mechanisms, I no longer choose the path of self-destruction.

And even when my marriage ended, I was not alone. I am never really alone. In Christ, I am a victor and no longer a victim. Peter wrote, "and He Himself brought our sins in His body up on the cross, so that we might die to sin and live for righteousness; by His wounds you were healed" (I Peter 2:24). My wounds were healed. I became victorious over the years of darkness and shame. And because of this, I have helped others become victors and victims no more since entering this field in 1977 upon graduating in psychology and theology from Palm Beach Atlantic University, and more since the recovery of 1985.

I love finding statements of victory. And one I couldn't agree with more is what my dear friend and fellow *The Chosen* fan, Dr. Benish Masih, posted in her biography, "The amazing news of the Gospel is not that we can receive Jesus into our lives. But He's already received us into His." It was very providential how I met her on October 13, 2020, and seen how the Lord has her minister to those of the persecuted church, those traumatized for their faith in Christ and in need of healing.

Five years earlier, in March 2015, at 59 years old, I had quadruple bypass open heart surgery at Liberty Hospital in Liberty, Missouri. The surgery was a serious one, lasting 13 hours. During my recovery in the ICU, the surgeon came to talk with me to transfer me to the regular unit. After some niceties, he cut right to it.

"You had the arteries of an 80-year-old," he told me.

I was not surprised. "Yep," I said, "That makes perfect sense to me."

Not expecting that reaction, he asked me why I felt that way.

I replied "My ACE score is 7, which, according to research, is high enough to take 20 years off of my life."

He asked for more information, and I launched into a mini-lecture similar to the ones I give to my college classes about ACE research and findings into the health risk of reducing average life expectancy.

You see, a large majority of people in America have an ACE score of 1 to 4. The good news is that, at these lower levels, no quality of life nor quantity of life reduction occurs. However, for each point between 4 and the highest score of 9, significant quantity and quality of life reduction occur. So, I wasn't surprised that my 59-year-old arteries looked like 80-year-old arteries to the surgeon who operated on me. After my talk, he took my hand and squeezed it.

"Well, I have given you your 20 years back," he said.

Upon hearing his words, I wept.

This kind of transformative healing is what I desire for you. I want the Lord to restore to you what the enemy has taken. I am a big proponent of guided journaling, like I have written in my Best Ideas book. Please consider what ACE events the Lord wants you to journal out. Consider the events that you have hidden in the basement of your soul. Do not keep them chained down in your soul any longer. Bring them into the light of day for healing.

I have a physical trainer, Dylan, who, with his sweetheart, Susie, are the best neighbors a guy could have. Except when he transforms into my trainer aka Punisher. He helps me find the discipline to perform lunges, wall sits, and weight lifting to transform my pain into muscle gain and weight loss. My goal is to get my soccer body back. Despite my sweat and tears, he tells me it will take another five years to get there. At least there is hope.

You see, the Lord transforms our hurt into hope. Whatever we have been through, Romans 8:28 applies. "And we know that God causes all things to work together for good to those who love God, to those who are called according to His purpose."

Alcoholics Anonymous and Celebrate Recovery groups work best when coaching in relational intimacy. No coach, except the Holy Spirit, is perfect, and some of the best sports coaches were not as good as players. Some of my best soccer coaches never even played the game.

So, it is with me in coaching you in this book. The Lord first gave me these ideas for this book years ago. I reminded Him of my past, which included two marriages in my twenties, one in my thirties, and one in my forties. I married a woman in my forties, which lasted for twenty years. But four divorces are a lot. The point is that the Lord took my injuries and turned them into hope for me. And now, I can use my healed wounds to help others.

Jesus In Samaria

John Chapter 4 tells about the time Jesus was in Samaria. His disciples had some errands to run in town and so left him on the outskirts near the well. A woman approached the well, and he asked her for water. She was surprised by this because she was a Samaritan, and they did not associate with Jews, nor Jews with them. They chatted for a bit, and then he prophesied about her having had five husbands. She was shocked, of course, and wanted to hear more. Their discussion centered around the well that went back thousands of years to Jacob and the water. Finally, He said, "If you knew the gift of God, and who it is who is saying to you, give me a drink, you would have asked Him, and He would have given you living water" (John 4:10). She was amazed by this and all that he knew. She rejoiced at what Jesus said and at His acceptance of her. We love much as we have been forgiven much.

Another woman we read about in Luke 7:47, "For this reason I say to you, her sins, which are many, have been forgiven, for she loved much; but the one who is forgiven little, loves little." Both of these women were living with burdens or darkness, but Jesus redeemed them out of His love. I can relate.

Overcoming Childhood Abuse

When I was meditating and preparing to write this book, I reminded God of the abuse I endured in childhood. Obviously, He didn't need reminding, but it was a way for me to communicate and talk with Him. As I communed, our conversation went deeper into my misuse of alcohol and how I used it and drugs and sex to self-medicate. It was His turn for a reminder as He led me to Isaiah "Lo, for my own welfare I had great bitterness; it is You who has kept my soul from the pit of nothingness, For You have cast all my sins behind Your back" (38:17).

When I lost my way in this manuscript, He encouraged me, "Write on." I have made so many mistakes along the way in my life and made thousands of wrong choices. But among the biggest was my choice *not* to listen to His voice when I knew better.

Plagued with a memory like mine, where I remember things I would like to forget and forget things that I would like to remember, it's hard to offer myself any grace. See the betrayal of trust in childhood abuse makes it quite difficult to trust even

God. That is why I believe childhood sexual abuse is Satan's best weapon to destroy lives.

I asked the Lord to bring me healing in this area. I asked for Him to infuse me with healing from hurt. I had burned myself to ashes many times in my life; I was usually the one holding the match. I knew He could transform my ashes into beauty and turn my mourning into joy. That was His mission statement that He read at the inauguration of His ministry here on earth, and I believe ours as well:

> "The Spirit of the Lord God is upon me,
> Because the Lord has anointed me
> To bring good news to the afflicted;
> He has sent me to bind up the brokenhearted,
> To proclaim liberty to captives
> And freedom to prisoners;
> To proclaim the favorable year of the Lord
> And the day of vengeance of our God;
> To comfort all who mourn,
> To grant those who mourn in Zion,
> Giving them a garland instead of ashes,
> The oil of gladness instead of mourning,
> The mantle of praise instead of a spirit of fainting.
> So they will be called oaks of righteousness,
> The planting of the Lord, that He may be glorified"
> (Isaiah 61:1-3).

Verse three says, "giving them a garland instead of ashes." This trade is what I wanted from God. I wanted to celebrate my life, all the bits of it, because He transformed my brokenness into something celebratory. I think that's what all Christians seek. We want Him to be glorified in and through us. It is not about me; it is about Him. If we allow Him access into the basements of our soul, we will do His good work within us. John wrote in Revelation, "Behold, I stand at the door and knock; if anyone hears My voice and opens the door, I will come in to him and will dine with him, and he with Me" (3:20).

What a beautiful picture of relational intimacy. Open the door to Him. Fling it wide open. There is joy in the morning. He has erased our walk of shame. I live in a No Shame Zone in Christ.

Past Pains

Yes, my childhood held some deep pain. My reaction to that pain was to escape through drugs, alcohol, and sex. Trauma in response to trauma. But the Lord has healed all the pain and suffering from my life, and through my experience of healing (my school of grace), He prepared me to teach others with similar stories.

He began his work in me at my college graduation in 1975. Actually, He intervened even before that when I switched colleges and majors from an electrical engineering major in a school in Atlanta, Georgia, to a double major in psychology and theology in a school in West Palm Beach, Florida. That was another example of a miracle of how the Lord had led me even when I did not have a clue what was going on.

At 21, I was athletic, quite a dancer, and plenty cocky. I thought I knew everything. But in the background, God was with me, guiding, nudging, and challenging.

After graduation, my first real job was in a group home for abused and neglected children. I didn't yet connect my past with theirs, but God knew. He opened my eyes to the world of hurt and suffering far greater than I had experienced. It was here, in this group home, that I learned I was not alone in living a painful childhood. Up to that point, I thought everybody else held aces, and I was dealt a lousy hand. My calling of setting the captives free became clearer as I formed and shaped my meaning and purpose in life to help people find relational intimacy with God, self, and others.

While in college in Atlanta in Electrical Engineering, I volunteered at the 700 Club Prayer and Counseling Center in Atlanta, Georgia. That turned out to be an unexpected blessing. I was paired with a godly saint and mentor, Cora Vance. She was the first to recognize my gift as a counselor and prayer warrior.

There were not many Christian counselors in America at that time. Bruce Narramore, who had and since has authored many books on Christian counseling and theology, and James Mallory, M.D. were the main ones at that time. Dr. Mallory wrote the book, *The Kink and I: A Psychiatrist's Guide to Untwisted Living*. Cora Vance gave me that book as a gift, and I devoured it. It profoundly affected and blessed me.

A few years later, when I went to seminary, I knew I was to be a Christian counselor, but not a pastor. I wanted to work with individuals and families to help them deal with abuse and neglect. I studied for two years in a master's of divinity program at Southern Baptist Theological Seminary in Louisville, Kentucky, before the Dean, Harold Songer, advised me to transfer to a psychology degree. I followed his advice and transferred to Nova University in Fort Lauderdale, Florida. All along, in the whispers of my life, God urged and guided me with mentors and people in authority who took an interest in me. My coming to you through this book results from the relationally intimate relationship with

Him, which led to fellowship with others just like in the first century Church.

The Descent

The descent from a psychology grad student to a drug dealer, even after the Baptism of the Holy Spirit years in Fort Lauderdale, Florida, happened very fast. It was the early 80's, and I was living and attending school in Fort Lauderdale, Florida. Someone offered me cocaine, and though I had heard that anyone who tries it becomes addicted, I tried it anyway. Hey, after all, Freud did it. Very soon, I regretted it. I felt like Adam and Eve must have felt in the Garden after they sinned.

I was a Christian, yet I still tried it thinking that cocaine was just caffeine on steroids. I quickly consumed line after line until enough was never enough. When I ran out of money I received a job offer. The job title was drug dealer, and no application was required. No background check, just the ever-present threat that if you screw up, you get shot, or chopped up with a machete and dumped in the Everglades. The insanity was that I was a master's level psychologist helping people by day and hurting them by night made me want to die. I wanted to divorce myself, otherwise known as suicide.

I could not stop upping the dose of cocaine or upping the risks of dealing.

I fell in love with a girl I had just met and thought I might move to Kansas City, her hometown. I fell into the old geographic-relationship cure that never works. *But how would I fund the move?* I wondered. *Oh, I know, I could mule the product from Florida to Kansas City!* I was intimidated away from the Lord by my own stupid choices. Relational intimacy with Him was not even on my radar! If I had been intimate with Him, I would have never entertained such insanity and sin.

Fast forward to October 1, 1985, when the Lord reached over and pulled me out of the sewage I was swimming in! Notice I said *reached over* and not *reached down*! In my own story and in the stories of many clients and friends I have been honored to know in my time, Jesus was there with us in the waste pond we chose to swim in, and at one point of despair, He reached over and said, "I love you, that is enough!" Then, He lifted us out of the miry clay and set our feet on the rock of our salvation!

I have not used alcohol, cocaine, or any other substance besides caffeine since October 1, 1985! He gets all the credit, honor, glory, and praise. I know I must stay relationally intimate with Father, Son, Holy Spirit, myself, and 5 to 7 others for the joy to continue! It is never easy, but it does get easier.

Hearing God's Voice

Several decades later, I was east of Saint Louis driving along Highway 100 north of Alton, Illinois, seeking God's will at that time in my life. The road runs beside the mighty Mississippi River on one side and huge white cliffs on the other. I watched the currents in the river swirl and dance at a vast place on one side of my car and the tall white cliffs on the other side. I was hedged between these two magnificent creations and humbled by God's majesty. But there was danger as well. If I swerved even slightly to the right, I would plunge into the river. To the left, I would smash against the rock cliffs. I began crying to the Lord, asking Him to reveal His will in my life. This book concept was ten years old at the time, and I was teaching and counseling the concepts in classrooms, seminars, and churches. I was still struggling with its application and how to scale it for a larger audience. I knew my beliefs and ideas could help many more people than I was currently reaching. But, at the same time, beneath my confidence, I felt most unworthy and unqualified. I sensed the Lord's still, small voice saying, "See how you cannot turn to the left or the right on this road? So, at this time in your life, you must keep doing what you are doing. Place one in front of the other on a straight path. Do not waver side to side."

After I heard His voice, my brain jumped to an incident that had occured in my early teens. I had been out camping in the Everglades with a group of mates. I wandered away from base camp as the sun was setting. I must have lost track of time because when I returned to myself, the sky was pitch black and I could not see anything. I couldn't even see the ground in front of my own feet. I was scared. But I felt a little comfort sweep through me and knew that God was with me.

"Put one foot in front of the other," He told me that night.

I did as I was instructed and found my way back to the warmth and welcome of the camp.   So, His message to me in the car was not new. He had spoken these words before. I had heard His voice before when I was much younger, probably ten years old. I was fishing with a buddy at Sawgrass National Park, also part of the Everglades. Fishing is a tranquil activity until it isn't. We had been casting for a bit when we set our poles down with the lines trailing lazily in the water. Suddenly, my pole took off through the water.

I did as any ten-year-old boy would do and jumped in the water after my pole. My mistake can be forgiven due to my youth, but that water was dangerous. It had alligators and snakes and appeared to be bottomless. It was a deep dark lake, and when I jumped in, I was wearing my waders, very heavy water boots. I immediately began to sink. I was terrified, frothing up the water, unsure how I would save myself from this one.

All of a sudden, I heard Him whisper, "I've got you." I wasn't startled by the voice, but I was about to go into shock. Suddenly, I felt my body lifted out of the dark water and gently placed back into our canoe. My buddy stared at me, his eyes wide with wonder, his mouth gaped open. He looked into my face, which mirrored his own. Something unnatural and unexplainable happened to me there in the water. My friend stood as testimony to the event.

I believe my guardian angel rescued me that day. There seemed to be no other explanation. Even if I had managed to swim back to the canoe, there was no logical way to get in it without tipping it. My boots were filling with water and the bottom of the lake was legions below me, and I would have no way to kick off from it for momentum. God truly does work in mysterious ways. The Psalmist writes, "They have seen his works in the Lord and his wonders in the deep" (107:4).

Although I was dripping wet when we arrived back at shore, my father did not mention my appearance. I told him I lost my pole and went after it but could not catch it. And this wasn't my first brush with death. My parents had almost one time before when I was two and enduring all those surgeries and fevers. But I had survived to the ripe age of ten and nearly died again. But ten would be a harrowing age for me. Later that same year, I ran into a post of a metal H-shaped unwrapped goal post on the goal line back then, during an informal school yard football game while going out for a pass, looking up over my shoulder for the ball. I had my tongue out, straining for the ball, and slammed into the pole with such force with my chin that I bit off my tongue and had a concussion.

My parents rushed me to the hospital. My tongue was only attached by a small amount of tissue and I was holding it in place. The doctor, perhaps to smooth my nerves, joked, "What's the matter, the cat got your tongue?" I attempted, though my tongue in my hand and the blood that wouldn't stop running, that no, the cat hadn't got my tongue; I had it right here. That night I almost choked to death on my blood in my sleep. My parents were watching me, ready with warm water to pour into my mouth in case I started choking and coughing on the blood. After sewing my tongue, the doctor instructed my parents to watch me through the night. It was one of the few times in my life that I did not talk too much.

God Will Bring Healing

Spend time with the Lord and listen to His voice and enjoy His beauty and wonders. He will make sense of all the pain and misadventures we have experienced, even if some of that pain is deep. My darkest pain centered around the abuse I received from relatives and strangers. Then I created a darker hole when I attempted to escape that pain through alcohol and drug use. So I had a lot of work to do with God to become a glorious creature in Christ.

The choices I made as a young adult rest solely on my shoulders. I was reacting to incidents that occurred when I was powerless, yes. But God, in His love, never violates our will. That means that bad things do happen to all of us. Humans hurt humans and God brings healing.

In counseling others and learning from them, I have found ways to bring healing to their trauma. My vocation is such a wonder. I have the privilege of counseling others, and, at the same time, my clients and students teach me as much as I teach them.

I once was honored with the responsibility of helping two parents who walked through their lives like Jacob Marley in the Christmas Carol, chained by the intense trauma of their childhood. I helped them cut the chains and watched them live free until they departed to Heaven. Now they are enjoying the presence of the Lord in their mansions. I have learned to accept healing myself to focus on the Lord's boundless love and His ubiquitous joy.

Chapter Twelve

Celebrate!

Taking Assessment

"I tell you that in the same way, there will be more joy in heaven over one sinner who repents than over ninety-nine righteous people who have no need of repentance" (Luke 4:17).

Celebration in Heaven must be so glorious. Reflect upon the process of the principles and activities of the last few weeks. Are there some things you would have liked to have done differently? That is a good sign as it shows growth. Having joy by being on the same page with your partner begins with a *yes* to the Lord and learning to be relationally intimate with God as Father, Son, Holy Spirit, ourselves, and others. Remember, He will not violate us. He stands at our door and knocks; it is up to us to open the door and say *yes*. He is always there waiting.

Practice - Taking Assessment

List five things you have learned through this book.

Write down five things you enjoyed about completing this book with your Same Page Partner.

Create a vision statement for what you believe God has for you.

Create a mission statement for your life.

Fill in the table in your Workbook with your short-term goals specific to the areas listed.

When I look up at the stars, I sometimes believe that some are dancing. God is a God of joy and whimsy. He created us with the ability to play and find joy in the ordinary. Play is an expression of the joys of life, the joy that is life. Trauma makes it hard to play, as Adam and Eve found out in the Garden of Eden after they disobeyed God. We have to learn to play again in the way the Lord has provided for us, and that can only come through our willingness to allow Him access to our deepest pain. When we learn to look, we begin to see His life is in us and all around us. His joy is evident. He truly will transform our mourning into joy. Together with your Same Page Partner, He will create beauty from ashes.

Closing Prayer

Lord, we thank You for all You've done for us now and through our lives. You brought us through so much. We ask You to help us take every thought captive and look out the new window that You provided for us. Give us the ability to serve and love You and others as we love ourselves. Lord, we pray for Your assistance and help in times of trouble. We ask that You take away the shame and show us the way of new life in Christ. I bless each one who reads this book and pray you guide them in their journey and bring people alongside them to love and nurture them into Your care. We thank You and praise You.

In the precious name of Christ Jesus we pray. Amen.

About the Author

Dr. Sarno is gifted in helping people find meaning and purpose in life. As a Christian counselor for over four decades, he specializes in helping people overcome addictions, anxiety disorders, and PTSD. A teacher at Liberty University Online, Dr. Al facilitates classes to help people find their zest for life. In his thriving practice, he counsels couples and provides them with the tools and techniques needed to instill joy in their relationships so they can live happy and fulfilled lives.

Dr. Al lives in Manhattan, Kansas, and is an active community member. His greatest joy is attending Rock Hills Church, where he loves to shout and sing praise to Jesus Christ.

You can reach Dr. Al at DrAlSarno.com.

Courses and Offerings

Dr. Al offers various self-guided courses on his website to help you build healthy and happy relationships. Some of the courses are:

- Using Your Brains - All Six of Them

- Six Types of Prayer

- Four Faces of Christ: Knowing Which Face to Wear When

- Bullseye of Balance for Healthy Relationships

- Moving from Toxic to Healthy Relationships

- Breathing Out Resentments, Breathing In Appreciations

And more!

You, too, can begin enjoying relationships. Simply enroll in a life-changing course today and learn the skills that Dr. Al has been teaching his clients for many years now.

Don't wait, ENROLL TODAY at DRALSARNO.COM

www.ingramcontent.com/pod-product-compliance
Lightning Source LLC
Chambersburg PA
CBHW052020030426

42335CB00026B/3224